Samuel Richardson and the theory of tragedy

Manchester University Press

Samuel Richardson and the theory of tragedy

Clarissa's caesuras

J. A. Smith

Manchester University Press

Copyright © J. A. Smith 2016

The right of J. A. Smith to be identified as the author of this work has been asserted by him in accordance with the Copyright, Designs and Patents Act 1988.

Published by Manchester University Press
Altrincham Street, Manchester M1 7JA, UK
www.manchesteruniversitypress.co.uk

British Library Cataloguing-in-Publication Data is available

ISBN 978 1 5261 1398 6 paperback
ISBN 978 0 7190 9793 5 hardback

First published by Manchester University Press in hardback 2016

This edition first published 2018

The publisher has no responsibility for the persistence or accuracy of URLs for any external or third-party internet websites referred to in this book, and does not guarantee that any content on such websites is, or will remain, accurate or appropriate.

Printed by TJ International Ltd, Padstow

For my wife, Nicola

Contents

Abbreviations	viii
Acknowledgements	ix
Introduction	1
Chapter 1	33
Chapter 2	64
Chapter 3	94
Chapter 4	120
Conclusion	154
Bibliography	162
Name index	172

Abbreviations

3C	Samuel Richardson, *Clarissa; or, The History of a Young Lady*, 3rd edn, 8 vols. (London, 1751)
C	Samuel Richardson, *Clarissa; or, The History of a Young Lady*, ed. Angus Ross (Harmondsworth: Penguin, 1985)
CL	Samuel Richardson, 'A Collection of the Moral and Instructive Sentiments, Maxims, Cautions, and Reflections, Contained in the Histories of *Pamela*, *Clarissa*, and *Sir Charles Grandison*', in *Samuel Richardson's Published Commentary on Clarissa*, ed. Florian Stuber and others, 3 vols. (London: Pickering & Chatto, 1998), vol. III
EW	Samuel Richardson, *Early Works*, ed. Alexander Pettit (Cambridge: Cambridge University Press, 2012)
P	Samuel Richardson, *Pamela; or, Virtue Rewarded*, ed. Albert J Rivero (Cambridge: Cambridge University Press, 2011)
SCG	Samuel Richardson, *Sir Charles Grandison*, ed. Jocelyn Harris, 3 vols. (Oxford: Oxford University Press, 1986)

Acknowledgements

My first acknowledgement goes to Jeremy Tambling, whose commitment as a teacher, scholar and friend will always be a model for me. I have also been helped by Hal Gladfelder, Daniela Caselli, Jeremy Gregory, David Punter, David Miller, and by the late P. N. Furbank. The initial period of research was supported by a grant from the Arts and Humanities Research Council. Thanks too to Manchester University Press for their interest and encouragement.

The earliest draft of this book was read and scrutinised by Joel Swann, and the final complete draft by Mareile Pfannebecker. Thank you both for that generous work. With these great friends – and with another great friend and influence, Alfie Bown – I hope there is a long conversation to come.

At the time when this book was contracted, I was helped a great deal by the hospitality of Lynne Harrowell and Richard Thompson in London, and Sam and Theo Austin and Mareile in Manchester. Cheers also to Leo Cookman, Matthew Judge, Mike and Michelle Collier, Naya Tsentourou, Dan Bristow, Paul Fung, Iain Bailey, Irene Huhulea, Colm MacCrossan, Andrew Rudd, Henry Power, and everyone at the Everyday Analysis Collective, #MCRPoetry, and Jeremy's theory reading group; as well as to my students at Manchester, MMU and Exeter.

My love and thanks go to my family: to my parents, Andrew and Wendy, to Lauren, to my grandparents, and to Ari and Diane.

Introduction

In the preface to the first edition of *Clarissa*, Richardson makes the familiar eighteenth-century gesture of reassuring his reader of the moral lessons the text is to impart:

> In the great variety of subjects which this collection contains, it is one of the principal views of the publication: to caution parents against the undue exertion of their authority in the great article of marriage: and children against preferring a man of pleasure to a man of probity, upon that dangerous but too commonly received notion, *that a reformed rake makes the best husband*. (C 36)

Clarissa's scope may be vast in addressing a 'great variety of subjects' and in being an epistolary 'collection' of different writers' letters and viewpoints, but it can nonetheless claim to be reducible to two main points of argument. Parental tyranny in the sphere of love is likely to bring misfortune, and young women shouldn't be fooled by the apparently attractive prospect of the 'reformed rake': the man who claims to have abandoned his days as a seducer while retaining the wit, manners and sensuality that allowed him to fulfil that role in the first place.

It is not unusual for authors of Richardson's time to begin their books by identifying certain follies in the world and to claim (with varying degrees of sincerity) that they have only written about them in order to put them right. But Richardson's preface is distinctive in intimating a quite specific process or mechanism by which those follies have come to be in first place. For Richardson, we might say, there must indeed be something 'dangerous' in the very way that public knowledge is constituted if such demonstrably false ideas can, through the various iterations they undertake in the culture, become 'commonly received': enshrined as truth, received wisdom or *doxa*. In this book, I should say from the start, I am less interested in the specific content of those ideas about tyrannical parents and reformed rakes than I am in the mechanism by which Richardson suggests they have perpetuated themselves.

The first argument of this book, then, is that Richardson's positioning his novel against the 'received notion' is not simply a passing remark in a conventional moralistic preface, but rather is one of the organising principles of the whole novel. I take it that whatever else it is, *Clarissa* is a diagnosis of a certain malignity in what we think of as common knowledge, or what Richardson sometimes refers to as 'public talk' (C 94). In *Clarissa*'s use of repetitions and quotations between and within the letters written by the novel's characters, Richardson seems compelled to show this dangerous 'public talk' at work, demonstrating how damaging ideas can become axiomatic simply by being repeated by the right people in the right way. We can say that the problem Richardson is analysing receives its parodic embodiment in a remark made by a man who speaks almost entirely in other people's proverbs, Lovelace's uncle, Lord M: '*what everyone says, must be true*' (C 606).

Once Richardson has made this analysis, the other challenge for his novel is to find some means by which to respond to or resist this problem of information. The privileged means – such is my book's second main argument – comes in the form of a figure of tragedy. Clarissa herself, by her unexpected and self-destructive resistance to the 'received notions' of her community, becomes the novel's greatest retort to them. This in turn effects a transformation not only in the way information is treated in the novel but also in the novel's own resources of representation: a transformation, I contend, that can rightly be called 'tragic'. To begin to sketch out this argument, this introduction does three things. First, it considers what it means for Richardson to turn to tragedy as a way of combating the dangerous situation of mediation into which the novel suggests discourse has been thrown. Second, it details Richardson's own arguments about tragedy in his fiction and conduct writing. And, third, it draws on nineteenth- and twentieth-century theorists of the disruptive power of tragedy to suggest how its importance to *Clarissa* extends well beyond Richardson's own sometimes contradictory statements about it.

I

Late in *Clarissa*, Lovelace's friend, John Belford, meditates on the phrase from Richardson's preface, '*a reformed rake makes the best husband*', and expresses concern for the 'many worthy women betrayed by that false and inconsiderate notion, raised and propagated no doubt by the author of all delusion'. Such women, he says, do not realise

> what a total revolution of manners, what a change of fixed habits, nay, what a conquest of a *bad nature*, is required to make a man a good husband, a worthy father, and true friend, from *principle*; especially when it is considered that it is not in a man's own power to reform when he will. (C 1393)

The rake's profligacy begins with his fallen state, and, while the Devil – 'the author of all delusion' – may lie about how easily that fall can be reversed and reformation found, it is too much inscribed in 'fixed habits' and repeated behaviours to be straightforwardly purged. True reformation, says Belford, would take nothing short of a complete transformation in identity: 'a total revolution of manners'.

The terms of Belford's argument are conventionally Christian, but the demarcation it makes between the part of subjectivity that is supposed to be inherent and the part merely produced in 'habit', as well as its interest in how the false information about 'reformed rakes' might have got around, puts it in line with the interests of a certain 'Enlightenment'. While it has become unfashionable to think of the eighteenth century as uniformly driven towards the principles of secularism, democracy and reason, Clifford Siskin and William Warner have argued that the category of the 'Enlightenment' nonetheless retains its usefulness if we take it as marking out the period as 'an event in the history of mediation'.[1]

This is to say that the seventeenth and eighteenth centuries were constituted by an unprecedented proliferation of means by which information could be dispersed, alongside an unprecedentedly detailed and adventurous cultural vocabulary for discussing those mediating processes of dispersal. In this view, the eighteenth century was not uniformly the 'age of reason' it has often been described as, but it did make the problematisation of knowledge, its provenance and its dissemination, its reigning conceit.

Clarissa's preoccupation with the dissemination of information and with the self-consciously mediated status of its epistolary form makes it consistent with this Enlightenment conceit. This interpretation finds support in the work of Mary Wollstonecraft, who seems to have Belford's remarks from *Clarissa* in mind in the section on rakes and women's attitudes to them in *A Vindication of the Rights of Woman* (1792). Whereas Belford's concern is with the aggressive rehabilitation required to rescue a rake, Wollstonecraft is more interested in what it is that makes women attracted to rakes in the first place. This is her more pressing 'revolution of manners', one concerned not so much with good and bad men as with the coordinates of female desire itself. 'In its present infantine state', she argues, feminine sexuality is little more than 'a set of phrases learned by rote', 'hackneyed in the ways of women', and, given the paucity of the culture supplying those phrases, it is unsurprising that in turn 'half the sex ... pine for a Lovelace'. 'Supposing', by contrast, 'that women were, in some future revolution of time, to become, what I sincerely wish them to be', Wollstonecraft says, 'even love would acquire more serious dignity', meaning finally that women 'would turn with disgust from the rake'.[2] For Wollstonecraft, a culture that consistently represents women as lascivious objects for men cannot subsequently be surprised to find the desire of its women interpellated by this representation in some way.

As with the moral claims of Richardson's preface, I am for now less interested in Wollstonecraft's specific views on problems in sexuality (as fascinatingly ambivalent towards their subject as they are) than in emphasising the mechanism of obscurely originating received notions by which Wollstonecraft proposes those problems have come about. Wollstonecraft's subtle adaptation of Belford's words from *Clarissa* raises Richardson's intuition about the dangers of 'public talk' to the level of an explicit, and newly feminist, political programme. But what, for either author, is the way out of this deadlock when, quite apart from knowledge and information conventionally defined, even the deep subjective reaches of desire itself are coded by dangerously self-confirming 'phrases learned by rote'? 'If such be the force of habit', as Wollstonecraft puts it, how are we to 'guard the mind from storing up vicious associations'?[3]

For Wollstonecraft and her circle, the meta-discourse that will get one beyond this fog of desire and hearsay is *reason*. Reason, imparted through education, will allow received notions to be circumvented and less damaging forms of desire to emerge. This radical kind of reason is one of the great democratic inheritances of the eighteenth century, and it is not going too far to say that it is the basis of modern critical thinking. What Wollstonecraft and her colleagues were practising was, at heart, a form of ideology critique: its central insight was that the areas of experience which appear to be outside politics are the most political spaces of all, and that which appears most intimately personal to us is the first thing that needs interrogation. But, at the same time, the terms available to Wollstonecraft clearly have their limits, and to address these we must have recourse to later tendencies in anti-Enlightenment thought.

If the keystone Enlightenment insight, that knowledge is not self-evident but is constructed and mediated in culture, is taken in all its radical force, what claim can reason have to rise above and speak over these other notions? Who is in a position to be so sure of themselves as to speak for what Wollstonecraft's compatriot Thomas Paine called 'common sense'? Certainly, the political duplicity of reason and common sense couldn't be any more clear today, when it is most often those on the right who appeal to them as a way of rejecting the supposed obfuscating abstractions or hopeless utopianism of left-wing intellectuals. The most polemical and important formulation of the wrinkle in reason's claim to clamber above the obfuscations of mediation and habit came from Friedrich Nietzsche. As Martin Jay summarises, whereas the Enlightenment radicals never quite abandoned their faith in a historically 'real' existence of reason somewhere beyond the mess of cultural mediation, 'Nietzsche's more radical gesture was to deny the premise of historical reality "in itself" ... All that was left was an irreducibly nontranscendental riot of interpretation without an external object to serve as the standard by which their veracity could be measured.'[4]

If this part of Nietzsche's argument is no doubt familiar to many readers, it is still worth emphasising just where he *does* identify truth if it is not to be found in some sort of transcendental reason or liberated common sense. In *The Birth of Tragedy* (1872), Nietzsche formulates an approach to truth that does not depend on Enlightenment reason, in what he calls 'tragic knowledge', a kind of knowledge with no final metaphysical referent outside what he calls 'eternal suffering and contradiction'.[5] Whereas the project of the Enlightenment radicals was to find in reason a truth that would redeem the contradictory distortions of culture, the articulation of tragedy is that the only available 'truth' emerges precisely from the gap of non-recognition between these areas of contradiction. I will explain what I mean by this a little more later on, but for now it is enough to say that as much as Nietzsche's association of tragedy with a traumatic 'other' kind of knowledge has been of constituent importance to subsequent critical theory, it can also be read backwards as part of the articulation of *Clarissa*. In *Clarissa*, Richardson had already intuited his own response to the deadlock of the 'received notion', which is different to the one Wollstonecraft later tried to use his novel to make. As with Nietzsche, the resources of response Richardson finds are not in reason but in tragedy.[6]

II

Richardson published the seven volumes of the first edition of *Clarissa* in three instalments in December 1747 and April and December 1748. Rumours began circulating after the publication of the second instalment that the novel's hitherto muted intimations of tragedy were to build to define its final three volumes. The revelation that the rake Lovelace was to do something that would place him beyond marriageable reprieve, and that Clarissa should die in the aftermath, provoked remonstrations from Richardson's circle of confidants, who had expected that the pair would finally be united in marriage.[7] As one critic remarks, Richardson seems to have been determined to 'challenge ... current notions of tragedy', even at the risk of 'social and financial liability'; in the words of another, he went as far as to consider 'the desire for a happy ending' among his readers as itself 'a mark of moral fault, an ameliorating concession to the religious laxity that plagued British culture at mid-century'.[8]

Richardson responds to the minor crisis the turn to tragedy presented for the serial publication of *Clarissa* in a postscript appended to its final volume. This begins by dramatically breaking the big illusion of all Richardson's novels: that the letters are real and that Richardson himself is merely their discoverer and editor.[9] Here, 'the author of the foregoing work' steps forward to describe the correspondence he has received from readers pleading that Clarissa and Lovelace be spared this dreadful mutual destruction. Richardson attributes their disquiet to the ongoing influence of the doctrine of '*poetical justice*', a seventeenth-century addition to the theory of tragedy developed in France but becoming influential to the point of being axiomatic in the English drama of the Restoration.

8   *Samuel Richardson and the theory of tragedy*

In *The Tragedies of the Last Age Considered* (1678), the critic Thomas Rymer had imagined a version of the birth of tragedy in which the genre was created by the Greeks to undo in art the moral mistakes of 'real' history:

> Finding in history, the same *end* happen to the *righteous* and to the *unjust*, *virtue* often oppressed, and *wickedness* on the throne: they saw these particular *yesterday-truths* were imperfect and unproper to illustrate the universal and eternal truths by them intended. Finding also that this unequal distribution of rewards and punishments did perplex the *wisest*, and by the *atheist* was made a scandal to the *Divine Providence*. They concluded, that a *poet* must of necessity see *justice* exactly administered, if he intended to please.[10]

In this analysis, tragedy is superior to the '*yesterday-truths*' of history because it secures a space in which dreadful actions and dreadful consequences neatly coincide in the same person: tragedy may represent the most wicked behaviour, but it also demands that it is punished in full measure. It was only, one might add, by logical tricks such as this that the genre traditionally most preoccupied with incest, murder and dismemberment could become what Timothy Reiss has called 'the ideal ordering and instructive mode'.[11]

For Richardson, appealing to poetical justice as a way of arguing against his killing the innocent Clarissa is inadequate on two grounds. First, its claims to being based in Christianity are decidedly shaky, demanding a worldly dispensation of punishment and reward that God never promised, for a mankind that has been placed here 'only in a state of probation'; God having 'so intermingled good and evil as to necessitate them to look forward for a more equal distribution of both' (C 1495). And, second, it is simply bad reading, misinterpreting Aristotle and great swathes of the canon of tragedies both ancient and modern, as the postscript quotes extensively from Joseph Addison's *Spectator* no. 40 in order to show. Richardson goes on to introduce the additional twist that, even given the inadequacy of the concept of poetical justice, justice actually *is* imparted to most of his characters, most particularly Clarissa herself, whose virtue 'HEAVEN *only* could reward' (C 1498). In this sense, Richardson is not among those modern commentators for whom Christianity and tragedy are diametrically opposed. On the contrary, if we push his view a little further, it transpires that while tragedy presents any number of examples of punishment far in excess of wrongdoing, it is Christianity that emerges as the truly tragic worldview, since its promise of justice after death actually licenses all kinds of injustice and cruelty prior to it. Much as tragedy in the French neoclassical dramatist Jean Racine's works is often thought of as an effect of God callously losing interest in man's worldly fate, true Christianity for Richardson is not there to offer consolation for tragedy but may even go as far as to produce it as part of its own internal logic.[12]

The alluring comparison between the *deus absconditus* of Racine and the worldview of *Clarissa* has been made in Leo Damrosch's book, *God's Plots and Man's Stories* (1985). In this analysis, the radical Catholic milieu of Jansenism that gave Racine his training and the English Puritanism that is often thought to have produced the English novel may not share much, but they do share a God who is fully willing to allow tragedy to occur in the world. What makes *Clarissa* formally 'post Puritan', in Damrosch's terms, however, is less any of its specific theological references or arguments than Richardson's employment of the epistolary form. Forgoing 'the normal basis of narrative, the presence of a teller and a tale', Damrosch argues, the 'editor' Richardson himself can be understood as 'a *narrator absconditus*', 'miming the hidden God who presides over the sublunary world but never shows his hand directly'.[13] In more recent criticism, the tragic dimension of this absconding of the ordering agency in Richardson's novels has been taken yet further, going bone deep into the characters themselves, who are no longer thought to be even the gods of their own behaviour. For Sandra Macpherson, *Clarissa* is full of actions, which, 'once begun', stubbornly refuse to 'come to rest' but insist on having disastrous effects quite contrary to the first intentions of their actors.[14] A similar insight underlies Jonathan Kramnick's reading of the novel through the lens of modern cognitive science as 'a series of questions about agency'.[15] Neither of these critics frames this specifically in terms of Richardson's discussion of poetical justice in the postscript, but it seems clear that there can be no dispensation of rewards and punishments according to moral worth in a universe where our actions do not come under our own control.

Richardson had not always allowed such tragic insight – or, indeed, patience for drama in general – so close to his writing practice. Before the explosion of *Pamela* established him as a literary celebrity, he had made a small but polemical contribution to what Thomas Keymer refers to as the 'new life' enjoyed by the old seventeenth-century campaigns to limit the freedoms of London's theatres, in a pamphlet called *A Seasonable Examination of the Pleas and Pretensions of the Proprietors of, and Subscribers to, Play-Houses* (1735), as well as in his conduct book for apprentices of the kind he employed in his own printing house, *The Apprentice's Vade Mecum* (1734).[16] These early pieces are reasonably conventional in calling for what he calls a 'double restriction' (EW 18) on taverns and playhouses as comparable sites of lechery and crime. More sophisticated are his arguments about the effects of play-viewing itself on the socially precarious young apprentices. With the exception of George Lillo's *The London Merchant* (1731) (a tragedy actually about an apprentice lured into vice by 'the artifices of a lewd woman' [EW 23]), Richardson argues that 'all our modern plays are calculated for persons in *upper* life, and the good instructions, if any are design'd to be convey'd by the representation to the mind of the auditory, lie much above the common case and observation of the class of persons to which I am addressing myself' (EW 19).[17] For Richardson, what goes on in the theatres is a pretty shameless example of what we would now call cultural hegemony: the plays enjoyed by a lower social group naturalise the worldview and concerns of a higher one. Worse, the Restoration plays still dominant in repertoire at mid-century assume a spectator who is explicitly contemptuous of the class and class values of the apprentices themselves: 'those written in a late licentious reign, which are reckon'd the best, and are often acted, are so far from being so much as *intended* for instruction to a man of business, that such persons are generally made the dupes and fools of the hero of it' (EW 20).

Even after Richardson's conversion to tragedy in *Clarissa*, something of the terms of his early antagonism to drama on social grounds remains. In 1753, the third and fourth editions of *Clarissa* were printed with a supplementary appendix entitled *An ample Collection of such of the Moral and Instructive SENTIMENTS interspersed throughout the work, as may be presumed to be of general Use and Service.* This was a different kind of conduct-writing to that which Richardson had produced before, a commonplace book collecting individual morally serviceable maxims from the novel itself and organising them under alphabetical thematic headings.[18] In 1755, Richardson published the *Collection* as a stand-alone text, accompanied by similar anthologies of quotations from both his first novel, *Pamela* (1740) and his latest one, *Sir Charles Grandison* (1753). Given what Richardson had staked on tragedy during the publication of *Clarissa*, it seems surprising to find in the *Collection* a return to the old suspicion of drama that had dominated his conduct-writing in the 1730s.

First off, *Clarissa*'s remarks about tragedy are compiled under the heading 'Comedies. Tragedies. Music. Dancing' (CL 100), putting the emphasis back onto the social entertainment side of drama as opposed to the aesthetic and ethical considerations that had dominated the postscript. This organisation also relegates tragedy from the privileged position it receives in *Clarissa*, forcing any reader interested in the topic to look first for 'Comedy'. These are the citations on comedy and tragedy given under this entry:[19]

> LIBERTINES love not any Tragedies, but those in which they themselves act the parts of tyrants and executioners. (C 618)
>
> Libertines (afraid to trust themselves with serious and solemn reflections) run to comedies, in order to laugh away compunction, and to find examples of men as immoral as themselves. (C 618)

> Very few of our comic performances give good examples. (C 618)
>
> Mr *Lovelace*, Mrs *Sinclair*, *Sally Martin*, *Polly Horton*, Miss *Partington*, love not Tragedies. They have hearts too *feeling*. There is enough in the world, *say they*, to make the heart sad, without carrying grief into our diversion, and making the distresses of others our own.
>
> The woes of others, well represented, will unlock and open a tender heart, *Lovel*. (C 620)
>
> The female heart expands, and forgets its forms, when its attention is carried out of itself at an *agreeable* or affecting entertainment, *Lovel*. (C 620)
>
> *Women, therefore, should be cautious of the company they go with to public entertainments.*

In the *Collection*, tragedy is made superior to comedy for its moral seriousness, while a preference for the escapism of comedy becomes an indicator of the wickedness of the libertine characters. Defending *Clarissa*'s tragic conclusion yet again in the revised postscript to the third edition, Richardson put the same charge to some of his readers, who, he says, 'declared against tragedies in general, and in favour of comedies, almost in the words of Lovelace, who was supported in his tastes by all the women at Mrs Sinclair's' (3C VIII, 278).

Despite this distinction, however, the terms of the critique of drama in general in Richardson's early conduct-writing remain, even if concerns originally raised about the class of the audiences have been reworked into ones about gender. Much as the earlier Richardson had warned that the theatre 'may entirely unhinge' an apprentice's 'mind from business', making 'music ... always play upon his ears' (EW 21), the *Collection* cites Lovelace to the effect that 'the female heart' is vulnerable to 'being carried out of itself' by the affecting spectacle of a tragedy. While tragedy is the genre favoured by virtuous women, it is also the genre that leaves them most vulnerable to manipulation by more powerful men: as much as the apprentices should be wary of the political implications of the plays they attend, women '*should be cautious of the company they go with to public entertainments*'.

On the face of it, this warning that glosses the quotations about drama in the *Collection* is a bit of a let-down. It appears that for all that Richardson's brilliant experimentation with tragedy in *Clarissa*, little had changed in his suspicion of drama in performance between the conduct books of 1730s and the 1750s. But such a reading only stands up until we use the page references Richardson added to the 1755 version to follow these passages back into the novel itself. The episode from which the warning about women going to the theatre is sourced is presented in Lovelace's Letter 194, which details his plan to take Clarissa to see a performance of Thomas Otway's Restoration tragedy *Venice Preserv'd* (1682):

> Whenever I have been able to prevail upon a girl to permit me to attend her to a play, I have thought myself sure of her. The female heart, all gentleness and harmony when obliged, expands and forgets its forms when attention is carried out of itself at an agreeable or affecting entertainment: music and perhaps a collation afterwards, co-operating. (C 620)

Women might well be advised to '*be cautious of the company they go with to public entertainments*' if this is the kind of thing their men are plotting, but the more important point is that the novel actually gives remarkably little evidence that such plots are particularly effective. Earlier in the novel, Clarissa has written similarly of how young women's vulnerability to seduction is exacerbated by the pressure they are made to feel to be 'obliging': 'an undesigning open heart, where it is loath to disoblige, is easily drawn in, I see, to oblige more than it designed. ... One's heart may harden and contract, as one gains experience' (C 269–70). And, indeed, her description of the theatre trip to Anna Howe does suggest that she may at least have been fooled into thinking the play has had such an emotional effect on Lovelace, who she thinks was 'very sensibly touched with some of the most affecting scenes' (C 640). But as for *her* 'heart' being 'carried out of itself' or inclined 'to oblige more than it designed' in the way Lovelace hopes and Richardson fears, it simply doesn't transpire that way. In fact, the letters that follow the performance of *Venice Preserv'd* are utterly indifferent to whether the play has affected her or not.

In other words, the old conduct-book-style arguments about the dangers of the theatre deployed in the *Collection* are pointedly *not* supported by the very episode in the novel that the *Collection* claims illustrate them. Perhaps Richardson betrays his own misgivings about having elevated Lovelace's plan to the status of a generally applicable warning when he attributes the last two passages specifically to '*Lovel*', whereas the others are allowed to stand unattributed as transparent universal truths. Richardson never considered that his apprentices might approach the plays they enjoyed with critical distance enough to avoid becoming their 'dupes and fools' (EW 20), and it might well be that he assumes that, since we cannot all be Clarissas, most of us need his warnings about what goes on at the theatre more than she does. But either way, taken as they stand, one cannot avoid the interpretation of these texts that the novel is making its own protest of resistance against its reduction to its constituent maxims in the *Collection*. At this tragedy, Clarissa is not only to casually sidestep Lovelace's plan but even frustrates the assumptions of Richardson's own conduct writing.

III

Perhaps it should not be surprising that, isolated in this way, Richardson's individual statements about the moral positioning of tragedy, on stage or on page, do not altogether cohere. At a time when all the major synthesising attempts to make a consistent theory of tragedy had at least claimed to be classically rooted in Aristotelian principle, Richardson himself was aggressively making a virtue of his separation from the classical tradition. In the retreading of the debate between the ancients and the moderns in *Sir Charles Grandison*, and in his contributions to his friend Edward Young's *Conjectures on Original Composition* (1759), the Richardson of the 1750s aligns himself against the cultural centrality of the classics in a way that Ian Watt goes as far as to compare to the militancy of William Blake's anti-classicism.[20] Even when Aristotle and the ancient tragedians do come up as authorities in Richardson's postscript to *Clarissa*, it is only in quotations from the great handbook for an emergent and proudly vernacular bourgeoisie, *The Spectator*. I cannot help but suspect that this lack of Aristotelianism and solid classical grounding in Richardson's approach to tragedy is what – whatever Richardson's intentions – makes it so amenable to comparison with the anti-Aristotelianism of theories of tragedy since German Romanticism. In this section, I want to outline an understanding of tragedy based on such theories and to explain how I am going to use them to understand Richardson's practice of tragedy in *Clarissa* for the duration of this book.

In his compressed and mysterious 'Notes on the *Oedipus*' (1804), Friedrich Hölderlin claims that tragedy is always a genre of 'emptiness', 'interruption', 'caesura', or what he calls here 'the pure word':

> The tragic *transport* is essentially empty, and the most unbounded of all.
> Hence the rhythmic succession of ideas wherein the *transport* manifests itself demands a counter-rhythmic interruption, a pure word, *that which in metrics is called a caesura*, in order to confront the speeding alternation of ideas at its climax, so that not the alternation of the idea, but the idea itself appears.[21]

For Hölderlin, the truth of a tragedy is not simply to be decided by a choice of one of the 'rhythmic succession' of available hypotheses or interpretations its situation presents. It is not enough if we come away from *The Baachae* thinking that Pentheus had it coming to him when he honoured his own authority over Dionysius, or from *King Lear* feeling that the old man should have shown more humility from the start. Nor is it the case, as Hölderlin's contemporary and one-time friend Hegel had it, that truth emerges as the new 'synthesis' of various opposing but, in themselves, equally valid positions. Instead, the tragic articulation comes out of an insistence on the materiality of *the gap between positions* itself, a commitment to the hard moment of 'interruption', which Philippe Lacoue-Labarthe memorably refers to as a 'wound ... that does not heal and reopens constantly under the hand that would close it'.[22] This is why, for Nietzsche, Hamlet's delay in killing his uncle has nothing whatsoever to do with the usual psychologising explanations that he is too frightened to act for himself, or is sidetracked by procrastination. On the contrary, it is his delay, and not the final killing, that constitutes Hamlet's tragic heroism. When, at the start of the play, 'the time is out of joint', with everyone in a position of radical insecurity in relation to one another, to actually kill Claudius would smack of a kind of capitulating closure. In this respect, the least tragic thing about *Hamlet* is the massacre at the end, because it clears the way for the stabilising return of young Fortinbras. For the interim, at least, Hamlet's delay works at sustaining a gulf, in which, Nietzsche says, 'insight into the horrific truth, outweighs any motive leading to action'.[23]

In a very similar way, *Clarissa* is a tragedy in which nothing happens, but not just in the sense of the familiar reader's complaint that its length is spectacularly out of proportion with the handful of however dramatic episodes it narrates. Rather, *nothing* happens, in the material sense of 'nothing' the Lacanian philosopher Alenka Zupančič describes as 'a certain – rather ghostly – materiality of nothing ... insisting/emerging in the real, while being deprived precisely of its symbolic support'.[24] Situations are set up, expectations are raised, only for an all-too-material 'nothing' to take the place of the anticipated outcome, and Clarissa's neglecting to comply with the expectations of either Lovelace or Richardson's own conduct writing at the performance of *Venice Preserv'd* is only one relatively innocuous example of the weight the novel places on this. When, finally frustrated with Clarissa's obtuse refusal to comply with virtually any of his expectations, Lovelace drugs and rapes her, he reports the action to Belford with these peculiar words: 'AND now, Belford, I can go no farther. The affair is over. Clarissa lives' (C 883).

This 'I can go farther' is especially difficult to interpret. Does Lovelace mean that there can no longer be any 'affair' between him and Clarissa since whatever was authentic in their strange relationship was dependent on a subtle interplay of wills which he has now broken by violence? Or does it mean he is too ashamed to write any more about the 'affair' of the rape to Belford now it is done? At least one critic has suggested that the words are a veiled confession of impotence and that Lovelace was unable to go through with the rape at all.[25] Perhaps the more important thing, however, is the way in which Lovelace's confusing words give a material acknowledgement of the most famous caesura in the text itself. For this is also the point in the novel where the punctual reportage of every minor event by dated letters suddenly breaks down, and the rape itself goes unreported.

This is perfectly, if rather surprisingly, Hölderlinian and marks the point at which Richardson's stated interests in contesting received notions in the preface and in tragedy in the postscript can be said to come together. For what is an epistolary novel but a 'rhythmic succession of ideas'? Particularly one in which so many of the writing characters, from the Harlowe family to Lovelace, have been so sure of their own. Bonnie Latimer has remarked of the meandering ambiguity of the ending of *Sir Charles Grandison* that, while it is true that 'there is no firm conclusion', none is actually needed because the characters' 'probable fates ... are to be inferred from their behaviour to date'.[26] The situation in *Clarissa* is almost exactly the opposite. The 'speeding alternation' of inferences about Clarissa's 'probable fate' voiced by the novel's characters (and by some of its readers) are exposed for the facile received notions they are when they are met with the caesural intervention of Clarissa at the point of the rape. What makes the novel truly tragic is that, whatever Richardson's own famous battles over interpretation with his more roguish readers, the text itself is far less interested in our reasonably making the right choice between various competing ideas than in insisting on the materiality of the gap between them: marking the traumatic space where 'the speeding alternation of ideas' becomes suspended and naked 'pure word' of 'the idea itself' is allowed to stand.

We can better take stock of this with reference to two further quite different theories of tragedy which nonetheless have a common point of reference in Hölderlin's '*Oedipus*' notes. These ideas will be familiar to some readers but are worth describing in detail since I will be referring to them throughout the book. First, I consider the German Jewish philosopher Walter Benjamin, who judged that the 'fundamental significance' of Hölderlin's '*Oedipus*' notes 'for the theory of art in general, beyond serving as the basis for a theory of tragedy, seems not yet to have been recognised'. Benjamin's whole philosophy, with its habitual investment in the notion of a 'tiger's leap' into an unknowable and unanticipatable sphere of difference might be characterised as an exercise in such a recognition. In Benjamin's view, such opportunely disruptive caesuras are potentially everywhere in modernity, as likely to crop up in the repetitive jarring of factory machinery, an abrupt cut in a silent film or the jerky gait of a drug-addled poet as they are in the divine violence of communist revolution. It is simply a case of radical thought developing the ability to recognise these gaps when they are there, for they are prone to appear without warning, much like the Messiah in the Jewish tradition in which Benjamin's thought is so entrenched.[27]

This, so to speak, is Benjamin's politics of tragedy: as much as for Nietzsche's Hamlet, it means committing to the caesural gap of what he refers to as 'the expressionless' (*das Ausdruckslose*):

> In the expressionless, the sublime violence of the true appears as that which determines the language of the real world according to the laws of the moral world. For it shatters ... the false, errant totality – the absolute totality. Only the expressionless completes the work, by shattering it into a thing of shards, into a fragment of the true world, into the torso of a symbol.[28]

While Greek tragedy offers one iteration of this 'expressionless' in what Benjamin describes as its heroes' silent refusal to speak in the compromised language of the community, the figuration is more strongly embodied in that drama's creaky and maligned early modern counterpart: the baroque *Trauerspiel* of the German seventeenth century.[29] Of these, the plays of the scholar-statesmen of the Second Silesian School, Daniel Casper von Lohenstein, Andreas Gryphius and Johann Christian Hallmann, are Benjamin's focus, although he finds their favoured tropes registered in a great range of cultural corners of the European sixteenth and seventeenth centuries. Jane O. Newman has emphasised that these plays were originally performed as part of the education of Protestant schoolboys and were aimed at shaping them 'as male civil subjects destined for positions in the early modern administrative bureaucracies of the Holy Roman Empire'.[30] This goes some way to explaining their ostentatiously 'academic' scholarly learning because, whereas 'the Renaissance explores the universe', Benjamin contends, 'the baroque explores libraries', so much so that in some of these plays 'the corpus of notes ... rivals the dramas in length'.[31]

Their civil and political function also accounts for what Benjamin frames as one of the *Trauerspiel*'s characteristic objects of analysis: the figure of 'the sovereign'. As the German jurist Carl Schmitt argued, law can only function if it has at its centre a figure, whether real or symbolic, to whom its strictures do not apply: that is to say, who has the power to occupy or declare a 'state of exception'.[32] While Schmitt, later a member of the Nazi Party, intended this as an apology for emerging fascism, Benjamin had already employed a very similar formulation from a leftist perspective in his *Critique of Violence* (1921).[33] In the *Trauerspiel* book meanwhile, Benjamin reads Schmitt's analysis of the sovereign back into the seventeenth century's preoccupation with the figure of the tyrant, remarking that 'the function of the tyranny is the restoration of order in the state of emergency: a dictatorship whose utopian goal will always be to replace the unpredictability of historical accident with the iron constitution of the laws of nature'. But for Benjamin, the melancholic outlook of the baroque merely demonstrates how there is no such law of nature capable of redeeming the chaos of 'historical accident'. Unlike Schmitt's anticipated Führer, the Hamlet-like sovereign of the *Trauerspiel* 'reveals, at the first opportunity, that he is almost incapable of making a decision'.[34] As it must for the famous angel of history Benjamin saw in Paul Klee's painting, history in the baroque remains an unredeemed 'catastrophe' of 'piling wreckage'.[35]

For Benjamin, this has both a theological context and an aesthetic one. If Richardson's fairly benign personal Anglicanism has been seen to be belied by the more startlingly Calvinist implications of his fiction, the *Trauerspiel* is even more avowedly a form in which God has absconded from the scene, leaving its practitioners 'taken up entirely with the hopelessness of the earthly condition'.[36] For Benjamin, this is the inheritance of the Lutheranism of German Protestantism for which there is no 'divine plan of salvation' accessible to the living, only a 'bare state of creation' emptied of cosmic meaning.[37] But this is not to set up Protestantism as some sort of prototype for the modern atheist-scientific position that finally sees the world stripped of obfuscating transcendence, 'as it really is'. Rather, as Samuel Weber emphasises, this emptying 'only endows' that transcendence 'with an all the more powerful force', an 'otherness' reappearing 'even more radically as *allegory*'.[38] The aesthetic corollary of the peculiar cultural situation of the baroque, Benjamin's idea of allegory goes well beyond the conventional definition of 'saying one thing in the language or imagery of another' and extends instead to a whole 'allegorical way of seeing'. 'In the field of allegorical intuition the image is a fragment, a rune', says Benjamin, 'the false appearance of totality is extinguished. For the *eidos* disappears, and the cosmos it contains shrivels up'. The arbitrary relationship of an allegory to whatever it is supposed to communicate means that, unlike the 'symbolism' theorised by the Romantics, it cannot sustain a 'totality' between material language and transcendental idea. The fallout of this is that 'any person, any object, any relationship can mean absolutely anything else'.[39] We should be careful here not to mistake Benjamin's notion of allegory for a forerunner of a postmodernist relativism in which, semantically speaking, 'anything goes'. The point is not that meaning is blissfully liberated from logocentric stricture in allegory but that the weight of significance is now placed on the rather grim and all too material space of mismatch between statement and supposed meaning.[40]

In a celebrated passage, Benjamin explains this with reference to the *facies hippocratica* – the face as it appears in between the last moments of life and dying – and what he treats as the prototype of all allegories, the *memento mori* of the bare skull:

> Whereas in the symbol destruction is idealised and the transfigured face of nature is fleetingly revealed in the light of redemption, in allegory the observer is confronted with the *facies hippocratica* of history as a petrified, primordial landscape. Everything about history that, from the very beginning, has been untimely, sorrowful, unsuccessful, is expressed in a face – or rather in a death's head.

Deprived of either a reliable sovereign's myth-making decisionism or the plenitude of meaning that a belief in an interventionist God can lend itself to, the baroque subject's perception is radically materialist. The paraphernalia of destruction are not 'transfigured' or dignified as they are in, say, the Romantic storm paintings of a Turner. Those chaotic objects that seem to have lost their reassuring place in ordinary existence, as a skull has lost its human face, are not to be symbolically recuperated by having 'deeper' meaning attributed to them. Rather, for Benjamin, the materiality of this very loss – the gap between the object and its supposed 'human' purpose – is actually a precious thing that must be melancholically maintained. To do so is to undertake the melancholic 'state of mind in which feeling revives the empty world in the form of a mask, and derives an enigmatic satisfaction in contemplating it'.[41] This, finally, is the rather shopworn tragic heroism available to modernity. For it is the last vigil capable of understanding, *pace* Schmitt, that '"the state of emergency" in which we live is not the exception but the rule'; that the caesura is not to be thought of as a temporary suspension declared for the convenience of an opportunistic sovereign but as continual rupture at the heart of being.[42]

This book argues that much of what Benjamin's elaboration on the Hölderlinian caesura attributes to the baroque is equally pertinent to the even more belated and confused form of mid-eighteenth-century tragedy as Richardson practises it. But to understand the place of the caesura in *Clarissa* more specifically we must introduce a second twentieth-century engagement with Hölderlin's thesis. In seminars delivered over 1959 and 1960 entitled *The Ethics of Psychoanalysis*, the psychoanalyst Jacques Lacan considers the potential of Sophocles' tragedy *Antigone* as a text for rethinking ethics in post-war Europe. Discussing the play, he offers the following surreptitious translation of Hölderlin's words into his own characteristic idiom. For Lacan, Antigone is most of all a figure who 'evokes' a certain 'right':

> a right that emerges in the language of the ineffaceable character of what is – ineffaceable, that is, from the moment when the emergent signifier freezes it like a fixed object in spite of the flood of possible transformations ... it is to this ... that the unshakeable, unyielding position of Antigone is fixed.

Whereas for Benjamin, the caesura is a recurring trope, inscribed in every part of the melancholy patchwork of the *Trauerspiel*, Lacan identifies it specifically with a single character in classical tragedy. The importance of Antigone is her unyielding refusal to compromise on her desire, a character trait that makes her exemplary of Lacan's central maxim for ethical conduct: 'the only thing one can be guilty of is giving ground relative to one's desire'.[43]

The 'desire' in question has a very specific meaning within psychoanalysis. Certainly what we are dealing with here is not the 'pursuit of happiness' enshrined in the American Declaration of Independence, or a matter of 'finding what you really want', as is recommended in today's discourse of self-help and spiritual well-being. Rather, the dimension of desire that Antigone commits to is located in the machine-like underbelly of the desired objects that seem to motivate us: what Freud called 'the drives'. Freud argues in the *Three Essays on Sexuality* and later in *The Drives and Their Vicissitudes* that there is a distinction to be made between the objects we take as the focus of our desires and the motivating forces in which desire originates. While it is reasonably common for us to imagine desire as coming into being in response to our encountering some stimulating object – as when a cartoon character's eyes leap out of his head when he sees a beautiful woman – Freud insists that the object is actually only the 'most variable' dimension of desire, 'is not originally connected with it' and 'becomes assigned to it only in consequence of being peculiarly fitted to make satisfaction possible'.[44]

Satisfying objects come and go, but the 'driving' force of desire prior to this moment of 'assignation' is characterised by a bleak kind of continuity, as Lacan says, with 'no day or night, no spring or autumn, no rise and fall', only 'a constant force'.[45] The decidedly unlikely miracle of desire then, comes about when this identity-less force of 'drive' is allowed to lock on to a given object.[46] In Lacan's view, this is only allowed to happen by the intervention of the little shard of the extra-linguistic Real, which at the time of the *Ethics* seminar he refers to as 'the Thing'. Impossible to symbolise, 'the Thing' momentarily promises the subject that it offers the completion of the founding lack that has set her drive in motion in the first place. Hence the Lacanian formula for the work of sublimation involved every time we single out one of the sea of basically interchangeable objects as constituting the object of our desire: 'it raises an object … to the dignity of the Thing'.[47]

But what has this to do with either ethics or tragedy? First off, for Lacan, the Freudian account of the drives calls for the reorientation of every previous system of ethics. The drives' headlessly meandering relationship to their objects means that human desire is constitutionally resistant to its own fulfilment. The unpredictableness of object choice meanwhile, means that desire is in no way especially predisposed to the beautiful or healthy objects that would supposedly do us 'good'. Indeed, they are not even limited to actual 'objects' conventionally defined. In *Civilisation and its Discontents*, Freud posits that the very psychological glitches and symptoms which are part of all communal living themselves may become for a person 'substitutive satisfactions', weirdly materialised objects of unconscious enjoyment, even if they cause 'suffering in themselves or become sources of suffering for him by raising difficulties in his relations with his environment'.[48] This is why Lacan argues that the most distinctive ethical inheritance of the Enlightenment, the utilitarian demand for the 'greatest good to the greatest number', doesn't only need to be qualified by the predictable objection that 'my good is not the same as another's good'.[49] More damning is the fact that what I momentarily select as my 'good' may actually be a curiously externalised part of my own desiring constitution; or – because as Lacan famously puts it, 'desire is desire of the other' – those of other people.

For Lacan, the ethical problem of capitalist societies is that their subjects are encouraged to be bound to this ever vacillating drama of shifting objects of desire, this 'service of goods', while embarrassedly laying down any part of their desire that poses too much of a threat to their stable self-image of consistent identity. But, much as I am arguing that tragedy provided Richardson with a conceptual vocabulary with which to explore the possibility of the transformation of the very language of his society, Lacan contends that 'the good cannot reign over us all without an excess emerging whose fatal consequences are revealed to us in tragedy'. And this is where Antigone comes in. In contrast to human-all-to-human life under this 'reign of the good', Antigone's desire for the burial of her brother to the cost of all else is 'something uncivilised, something raw', going well beyond any conventional identity-confirming elevation of a given aim. Instead, behind Antigone's actions is a brute commitment to the drive itself, burning through the comfortably socialised 'object-ness' of her attachment until 'there is no longer any object', only the bleak inhuman 'Real' of the naked drive. This, finally, is the ethical lesson offered in tragedy. One does not resist the malignity of the 'service of goods' by laying down selfish desires in favour of the 'greater good' but rather by taking them to their very inhuman limit.[50]

Admittedly, for most of us, the momentary opportunity to behave ethically in relation to this desire-in-the-Real is not usually as dramatic or presented in such clear sight as Antigone's desire for the burial of her brother. It is not even always so in tragic drama. Antigone's quasi-incestuous transgression is often thought of as analogous to that of her father, Oedipus, who killed his father and slept with his mother. Is Oedipus' pursuit of his desire for Jocasta to the destruction of all else, then, an equivalently ethical refusal to 'give ground'? For Lacan, the truth is slightly more banal. Oedipus' unknowing incest may send him, like Antigone, 'beyond the sphere of the service of goods ... into the zone in which he pursues his desire', but it scarcely represents the same kind of heroic sacrifice as his daughter's, since Oedipus thought he was doing little more than settling into a conventional marriage having successfully avoided the destructive fate that had been predicted for him.[51] The way in which he does not 'give ground in relation to desire' is actually found in the more subtle detail of the way he acts *after* the terrible realisation has been made. Lacan notes that in the moment of his having lost everything, Oedipus nonetheless continues to behave in much the same way as he did before, haughtily demanding further answers from his various courtiers. This desire to know, which is usually thought of as marking all Oedipus' conduct up until this point, is retained even in the tragic space of the completely unrecognisable new constellation that it has created. It is in this rather more modest commitment to desire that Oedipus' ethical stance is located.

In *Antigone*, then, the dilemma over the burial of the brother presents only a rather elevated example of how the coincidence of a desire with an act that will overturn one's existing symbolic coordinates will always prompt the elementary ethical question: should I allow this desire to tumble metonymically into something more safely acceptable to the service of goods (as most of us usually do)? Or should I commit to my desire at the risk of losing all my recognisable subjectivity? *Oedipus the King*, meanwhile, offers a more everyday or even bathetically comic instance of this dilemma. For Oedipus, it is no longer a grand political gesture like the burial of a war criminal that produces this radically desired 'object' but an externalised element of his own desiring constitution. There is an analogous moment in Clarissa's Letter 82, written days before her abduction from Harlowe Place by Lovelace. There, she countenances the possibility that however justified her resistance to the marriage her family are forcing her into might be, there is also a sense in which both she and they are driven by a stubborn impulse not entirely limited to the situation at hand. 'We seem to be *impelled*, as it were, by a perverse fate which none of us are able to resist', she reflects to Anna, 'and yet all arising (with a strong appearance of self-punishment) from ourselves':

> your partial love will be ready to acquit me of capital and intentional faults – but oh, my dear! my calamities have humbled me enough to make me turn my gaudy eye inward; to make me look into myself! – And what have I discovered there? – Why, my dear friend, more *secret* pride and vanity than I could have thought had lain in my unexamined heart. (C 333)

At the same comparatively early point, Clarissa is already contemplating that her circumstances and this character trait may result in her death. 'I shall not live always! – May but my *closing* scene be happy!', she says in the same letter, adding later that evening that she has been made to reassure her family that she does not intend to commit suicide (C 341). We might expect this early indication of a potentially self-destructive trace of pride to be expunged by the novel in some sort of conventional life lesson. But in fact it will actually prove to be Clarissa's major and most important source of resistance: first to the Harlowes, then to Lovelace in his attempts to seduce her, and finally to Lovelace and his family's attempts to ameliorate the rape by having Clarissa marry him. As Lovelace will eventually remark, 'who the devil could have expected ... a lady so immovably fixed' (C 1290). Even at this early stage, the novel suggests that Clarissa's ethical resistance to such recuperations of the 'service of the goods' comes not simply from a higher plane of principle but, like Oedipus's, from an obscure part of her own desire: in psychoanalytic terms, from an inhuman commitment to the drive itself.

Terry Eagleton, among other critics, has referred to Clarissa as Antigone's 'English equivalent' and as 'another remarkable female figure of world literature who dies of refusing to relinquish her desire'.[52] This book shares Eagleton's intuition that Clarissa is for Richardson something analogous to what Antigone is for Lacan, even if Clarissa's desire is, like Oedipus', rather more obscure and submerged than Antigone's. The eighteenth century was surprisingly indifferent to representing the Antigone myth in its art and literature, and yet Richardson writes of a woman whose commitment to a dangerous dimension within herself precipitates a tragedy.[53] This is tragedy not as a mere cautionary moral fable but as an attempt to write in the very caesura of meaning and identity that Benjamin and Lacan were reaching for in the twentieth century. The chapters that follow flesh out the case I have made here, proceeding through the novel roughly in narrative order. Chapter 1 concerns Richardson's representation of the dynamics of the 'received notion', the constituting mechanism of public knowledge that he says he wrote the novel to contest. It shows how, in the novel's first instalment, the imprisonment and tormenting of Clarissa by her family is executed by their quotation and repetition of certain phrases or statements from either her letters or theirs. This process, which is also in evidence in the letters between the rakes, constitutes Richardson's diagnosis of the dangerously shifting grounding for public knowledge in the novel. Chapter 2 takes up the novel on the other side of its major caesural moment, Lovelace's rape of Clarissa, and investigates the remarkable set of fragmentary texts, or 'mad papers', she composes at this point. Here I am influenced by Benjamin's analysis of how quotations and allegorical images became eerily alienated from meaning under the melancholic gaze of the *Trauerspiel* authors, to show how the novel seems to register the new loss of effectiveness of the 'received notion' at the level of its form. Chapter 3 remains with the mad papers and their surrounding letters, drawing attention to how their problematisation of authoritative quotation extends to the strange way in which they are mediated in the transcriptions of other characters in the novel. This chapter also analyses Lovelace's psychologically fascinating response to the rape of Clarissa and argues that it is Clarissa's Antigone-like resistance to his attempts to reverse that tragedy that drives the latter stages of the novel. The landscape of the novel in its final volumes is the subject of Chapter 4, in which I show the relevance of Benjamin's analysis of the baroque to Clarissa's long approach to death. The Conclusion, finally, returns to the theories of tragedy discussed in this introduction, making a final Nietzschean 'attempt at self-criticism' of my theory of *Clarissa*, through the lens of Lacan's later work on sexual difference.

Notes

1 See Clifford Siskin and William Warner, 'Introduction', in Clifford Siskin and William Warner (eds), *This Is Enlightenment* (Chicago, Ill.: University of Chicago Press, 2010), pp. 1–36; see also John Bender, 'Novel Knowledge: Judgement, Experience, Experiment', in Clifford Siskin and William Warner (eds), *This Is Enlightenment* (Chicago, Ill.: University of Chicago Press, 2010), pp. 284–300.
2 Mary Wollstonecraft, *Political Writings*, ed. Janet Todd (London: William Pickering, 1993), pp. 202, 205–6; Wollstonecraft is adapting Shakespeare's words about a king who has failed to remain sufficiently aloof from the gossip of his subjects in *Henry IV, Part 1*: 'so common hackneyed in the eyes of men' (III.ii.40). Throughout this book, quotations from Shakespeare are referenced parenthetically by act, scene and line and are from *The Complete Works*, ed. Stanley Wells and Gary Taylor (Oxford: Clarendon Press, 2006).
3 Wollstonecraft, *Political Writings*, p. 206.
4 Martin Jay, *Downcast Eyes: The Denigration of Vision in Twentieth-Century French Thought* (Berkeley, Calif.: University of California Press, 1993), pp. 189–90.

5 Friedrich Nietzsche, *The Birth of Tragedy*, trans. Douglas Smith (Oxford: Oxford University Press, 2000), p. 30.

6 A recent article by Felicity A. Nussbaum suggests that his work was not alone in the century in making this choice. As she asks in 'The Unaccountable Pleasure of Eighteenth-Century Tragedy', *PMLA*, 129 (4) (2014): 688–707: 'if Enlightenment hope and faith in progress were not compatible with portraying tragic suffering, why did old and new tragedies continue to be produced on the eighteenth-century stage?' (p. 689).

7 This was reflected in the sales of the novel's final instalment, which came out at less than two-thirds that of its first two; see Thomas Keymer, 'Clarissa's Death, *Clarissa*'s Sale, and the Text of the Second Edition', *Review of English Studies*, 45 (179) (1994): 389–96; for Richardson's commitment to the tragic outcome from the earliest drafting stage, see E. Derek Taylor, *Reason and Religion in Clarissa: Samuel Richardson and 'The Famous Mr Norris of Bemerton'* (Farnham: Ashgate, 2009), pp. 1–2.

8 Adam Budd, 'Why Clarissa Must Die: Richardson's Tragedy and Editorial Heroism', *Eighteenth-Century Life*, 31 (3) (2007): 1–28 (p. 3); Alex Eric Hernandez, 'Tragedy and the Economics of Providence in *Clarissa*', *Eighteenth-Century Fiction*, 22 (4) (2010): 599–630 (p. 605).

9 For Samuel Johnson's irritation with Richardson's perpetuating this affectation even during the publication of *Sir Charles Grandison*, see *The Letters of Samuel Johnson*, ed. Bruce Redford, 3 vols. (Oxford: Clarendon Press, 1992), vol. I, p. 48.

10 Thomas Rymer, *The Critical Works*, ed. Curt A. Zimansky (Westport, Conn.: Greenwood Press, 1971), p. 22.

11 Timothy Reiss, *Tragedy and Truth: Studies in the Development of a Renaissance and Neoclassical Discourse* (New Haven, Conn.: Yale University Press, 1980), p. 9; see also Terry Eagleton, *Sweet Violence: The Idea of the Tragic* (Oxford: Blackwell, 2003), p. 138.

12 See Lucien Goldmann, *The Hidden God: A Study of the Tragic Vision in the Pensées of Pascal and the Tragedies of Racine*, trans. Philip Thody (London and New York: Routledge, 1964).

13 Leopold Damrosch Jr., *God's Plots and Man's Stories: Studies in the Fictional Imagination from Milton to Fielding* (Chicago, Ill.: The University of Chicago Press, 1985), pp. 213, 258–9.

14 Sandra Macpherson, *Harm's Way: Tragic Responsibility and the Novel Form* (Baltimore, Md.: The Johns Hopkins University Press, 2010), p. 61.

15 Jonathan Kramnick, *Actions and Objects from Hobbes to Richardson* (Palo Alto, Calif.: Stanford University Press, 2010), p. 194.
16 Tom Keymer, *Richardson's Clarissa and the Eighteenth-Century Reader* (Cambridge: Cambridge University Press, 1992), p. 143; on these, see also Rebecca Tierney-Hynes, *Philosophers and Romance Readers, 1680–1740* (London: Palgrave, 2012), pp. 141–4.
17 On Lillo's distinctiveness from the Restoration tragedies, see J. Douglas Canfield, *Heroes and States: On the Ideology of Restoration Tragedy* (Lexington, Ky.: University Press of Kentucky, 2000), pp. 171–5.
18 On Richardson's interest in the anthology form, see Leah Price, *The Anthology and the Rise of the Novel: From Richardson to George Eliot* (Cambridge: Cambridge University Press, 2000), Chapter 1; on the ongoing importance of the Renaissance tradition of the commonplace book in eighteenth-century culture, see David Allan, *Commonplace Books and Reading in Georgian England* (Cambridge: Cambridge University Press, 2010).
19 I have altered Richardson's volume and page references to refer to the Penguin Classics edition.
20 Ian Watt, *The Rise of the Novel: Studies in Defoe, Richardson and Fielding* (London: Chatto & Windus, 1957), p. 243.
21 Friedrich Hölderlin, *Essays and Letters*, ed. and trans. Jeremy Adler and Charlie Louth (London: Penguin, 2009), p. 318.
22 Philippe Lacoue-Labarthe, *Typography: Mimesis, Philosophy, Politics*, ed. Christopher Fynsk (Palo Alto, Calif.: Stanford University Press, 1989), p. 213; as he later elaborates on this: 'the tragic spectacle presupposes, behind it, the irremediable loss of every secure position and determination of enunciation' (p. 234).
23 Nietzsche, *The Birth of Tragedy*, p. 46; for another recent interpretation of this passage, see Simon Critchley and Jameson Webster, *The Hamlet Doctrine* (London: Verso, 2013), pp. 194–9.
24 Alenka Zupančič, *Why Psychoanalysis? Three Interventions* (Uppsala: NSU Press, 2008), p. 60.
25 Judith Wilt, 'He Could Go No Farther: A Modest Proposal about Clarissa and Lovelace', *PMLA*, 92 (1) (1977): 19–32.
26 Bonnie Latimer, *Making Gender, Culture, and the Self in the Fiction of Samuel Richardson* (Farnham: Ashgate, 2013), p. 191.
27 Walter Benjamin, *Selected Writings*, ed. and trans. Marcus Bullock and Michael W. Jennings and others, 4 vols. (Cambridge,

Mass.: The Belknap Press, 1996), vol. I, p. 340; vol. IV, pp. 393, 387.
28 Benjamin, *Selected Writings*, vol. I, p. 340.
29 Walter Benjamin, *The Origin of German Tragic Drama*, trans. John Osborne (London: Verso, 1998), p. 108.
30 Jane O. Newman, *Benjamin's Library: Modernity, Nation, and the Baroque* (Ithaca, NY: Cornell University Press, 2011), pp. 83–4.
31 Benjamin, *The Origin of German Tragic Drama*, pp. 60, 140, 63.
32 For a recent account of the Schmitt–Benjamin relationship, see Elizabeth Stewart, *Catastrophe and Survival: Walter Benjamin and Psychoanalysis* (New York: Continuum, 2010), pp. 1–4; and on Schmitt and the early modern period more generally, Graham Hammill and Julia Reinhard Lupton (eds), *Political Theology and Early Modernity* (Chicago, Ill.: University of Chicago Press, 2012).
33 See Giorgio Agamben, *The State of Exception*, trans. Kevin Attell (Chicago, Ill.: University of Chicago Press, 2005), pp. 52–3.
34 Benjamin, *The Origin of German Tragic Drama*, pp. 74, 71.
35 Benjamin, *Selected Writings*, vol. IV, p. 392.
36 Benjamin, *The Origin of German Tragic Drama*, p. 81.
37 For a full discussion of Benjamin's interpretation of Lutheranism and its sources, see Newman, *Benjamin's Library*, pp. 154–69.
38 Samuel Weber, *Benjamin's -abilities* (Cambridge, Mass.: Harvard University Press, 2008), p. 187.
39 Benjamin, *The Origin of German Tragic Drama*, pp. 166, 176, 175.
40 See Jeremy Tambling, *Hölderlin and the Poetry of Tragedy: Readings in Sophocles, Shakespeare, Nietzsche and Benjamin* (Brighton: Sussex Academic Press, 2014), p. 233: 'we can now align Hölderlin's caesura, and the expressionless, and the pure word, as analogous terms whose other name is Benjamin's "allegory"'.
41 Benjamin, *The Origin of German Tragic Drama*, pp. 166, 139.
42 Benjamin, *Selected Writings*, vol. IV, p. 392.
43 Jacques Lacan, *The Ethics of Psychoanalysis*, ed. Jacques Alain-Miller, trans. Dennis Porter (London: Norton, 1992), pp. 279, 321.
44 Sigmund Freud, *The Ego and the Id and Other Works*, ed. and trans. James Strachey (London: Vintage, 2001), p. 122.
45 Jacques Lacan, *The Four Fundamental Concepts of Psychoanalysis*, ed. Jacques Alain-Miller, trans. Alan Sheridan (London: Norton, 1998) p. 165.

46 'The miracle of desire' is Alenka Zupančič's phrase; see *The Shortest Shadow: Nietzsche's Philosophy of the Two* (Cambridge, Mass.: The MIT Press, 2003), p. 175.
47 Lacan, *The Ethics of Psychoanalysis*, p. 112.
48 Sigmund Freud, *The Future of an Illusion, Civilisation and its Discontents and Other Works*, ed. and trans. James Strachey (London: Vintage, 2001), p. 108.
49 Lacan, *The Ethics of Psychoanalysis*, p. 187.
50 Lacan, *The Ethics of Psychoanalysis*, pp. 305, 259, 263, 149.
51 Lacan, *The Ethics of Psychoanalysis*, p. 304.
52 Terry Eagleton, *Trouble with Strangers: A Study of Ethics* (Oxford: Blackwell, 2009), p. 206; for a similar passing comparison, see Damrosch, *God's Plots and Man's Stories*, p. 256.
53 On the virtually complete absence of Antigone from eighteenth-century art and literature, see George Steiner, *Antigones* (Oxford: Clarendon Press, 1984), pp. 6–7; and Edith Hall and Fiona Macintosh, *Greek Tragedy and the British Theatre: 1660–1914* (Oxford: Oxford University Press, 2005), p. 317.

1

Richardson's fictions were associated with representing reality with unprecedented convincingness early on. The villagers of Slough and Preston may or may not have jubilantly sounded the church bells on reading of Pamela's marriage to Mr B, but the significance of the anecdote's popularity in the eighteenth century is that it didn't seem implausible that they might have done.[1] Reflecting on *Clarissa*, the poet and dramatist Aaron Hill summed up this effect when he wrote to Richardson 'that we can find no difference at all, in the impression of things really done, and past, and recollected by us – and the things we read of, in this *intellectual world* which *you* have naturalized us into'.[2] But whatever Richardson's established place in the history of realism, his claim in the preface to *Clarissa* that his novel was written to diagnose and to overturn 'commonly received notion(s)' suggests that, as much as he wanted to invite readers to revel in the marvellous plausibility of his '*intellectual world*', he was also seeking to provide an interruption in the smooth running of the real world as it is. The operation of *Clarissa* was that it should leave its readers capable of standing critically apart from the more specious assumptions about gender, class, God and power doing the rounds in the world outside the text, even as they became more and more absorbed in the minute dilemmas and exercises of feeling going on inside it.

The rest of this book will show that as *Clarissa* develops it increasingly raids the archive of tragedy for alternative forms of expression and knowledge to such conventional received notions. But prior to this tragic turn, Richardson spends a considerable amount of *Clarissa*'s first instalment demonstrating how those received notions managed to gather the authority and the appearance of truth they had in the first place. Let us take the key example of a received notion as Richardson uses the term in the preface: '*a reformed rake makes the best husband*' (C 36). In the novel's earliest letters, Richardson is already showing how that maxim has been allowed to take hold. In her first letter, Clarissa describes her elder sister Bella's attitude to Lovelace during his initial courtship of Bella. She regarded him as 'wild', Clarissa writes, '*very* wild, very gay; loved intrigue. But he was young; a man of sense: would see his error, could she but have patience with his faults, if his faults were not cured by marriage' (C 42). Lovelace surprises Bella by taking her conventionally coquettish rejection of his initial advances at its word and, in pretended disappointment, begins to court the younger sister instead. If the family's first hope was that, whatever rakishness there was in Lovelace's youth it would soon be 'cured by marriage' to Bella, that idea gets neatly transposed to this second love interest. As the sisters' uncle remarks, Clarissa 'would reform him if any woman in the world could' (C 45).

At the start of the novel, then, the 'dangerous ... notion' that Lovelace's rakishness is a small price to pay for his charm and status and, anyway, will subside after marriage to one sister or the other, does indeed seem to be 'commonly received': although not especially – as one might have thought – by the impressionable adolescent girls Clarissa and Anna themselves. It is an unpleasant irony of the Harlowe family's quickly escalating cruelty against Clarissa that the courtship with Lovelace that supposedly motivates it is initially more welcomed by them than by her. Indeed, when Lovelace comes to petition Anna to speak to Clarissa in his favour, by contrast, Anna's reply is a precise reversal of '*a received rake makes the best husband*': 'it was surprising that young gentlemen, who gave themselves the liberties he was said to take, should presume to think that, whenever they took it into their heads to marry, the most virtuous and worthy of the sex were to fall to their lot' (C 216). Richardson's examination of how spurious notions come to be regarded as truth is, it seems, to be rather more sophisticated than simply having his protagonists fall for them.

In *Clarissa's Ciphers*, Terry Castle emphasises that part of what is so disturbing about the control Lovelace comes to exercise over Clarissa once he has abducted her is that it goes beyond the merely physical, extending to the very language and conceptual vocabulary available to her for processing her experience. 'Metaphoric aggression', Castle suggests, is 'Lovelace's first and most basic affront against Clarissa. It becomes the prototype for every other kind of abuse he wages against her', whether in presenting false personae of himself and his confederates, lying about their geographical location, or – most disastrously – finally assuming to interpret and to speak for her desire itself in the rape. But if Lovelace is endowed with special linguistic gifts that allow him to succeed for a time in these kinds of invasions of Clarissa's language, he by no means has a monopoly on 'linguistic persecution'. In fact, says Castle, in the novel's first instalment, Clarissa's family's 'persecutions prefigure those of Lovelace', as they work hard – if not always successfully – to deprive Clarissa of the ability to write or to contact any sympathetic interlocutors.[3]

This chapter builds on Castle's insight that the first instalment of *Clarissa* is dominated by linguistic persecutions imposed on Clarissa by the Harlowes in a manner that anticipates the violence that is done to her by Lovelace. If it does depart from Castle, it is in arguing that the form such linguistic persecutions take is sometimes even more blunt and heavy-handed than her analysis implies. I want to show that the Harlowes' bullying attempt to force compliance from the intransigent youngest daughter provides Richardson with an opportunity to show his idea of the received notion in action. Rumours, maxims, old bits of folk wisdom and quotations from other texts crowd the letters of the novel's first volumes, demonstrating how ideas can gain or lose the appearance of truthfulness depending on how and how often they get quoted or retold, and by whom. The Harlowes, it seems, are old hands at this, and at several charged moments their persecution of

Clarissa explicitly takes the form of quoting from each others' letters and statements in order to build them up into accepted truths; or otherwise quoting Clarissa's own words back to her in such a way as to discredit them. The chapter, then, begins by considering the different forms the received notion takes in the first instalment, starting with the sideways glances the text makes to a building culture of rumour surrounding the goings on at Harlowe Place and the extent to which the epistolary form itself might be implicated in such a culture. Second, it examines the Harlowes' linguistic persecution of Clarissa at work, showing how their letters allow particular attitudes to build up into full-blown received notions. And, finally, it turns to Lovelace and the rakes, whose libertine behaviour is represented by Richardson as being less a spontaneous acting upon animal urges than a carefully structured set of behaviours enacted in accordance with – once again – certain maxims that gain their authority by being repeated.

I

Richardson's novel is dominated by the writing voices of the small group of characters whose letters we actually get to read, but it also periodically draws our attention to a chattering culture of rumours about those characters situated just within the text's peripheral vision. This, I argue, is Richardson's first examination of the way received notions are created and reinforced by repetition within a culture, and it begins with a consideration of the 'fame' Clarissa is said to have at the start of the novel. In a recent study, Philip Hardie emphasises what he calls the 'duplicities' of the concept of fame, originating in the fact that in classical times the term *fama* could refer simultaneously to stories of the acknowledged exploits of great individuals, as well as to the more scurrilous and unstable circulation of misinformation about them.[4] By Richardson's day, English literature had already made substantial engagements with this ambiguity, for instance at the start of the second part of Shakespeare's *Henry IV* (1596), in which Rumour appears on stage to spread misinformation about the actions of the heroes at the end of the previous play. A few years later, in *Poetaster* (1601), Ben Jonson recast the struggles of fame and slander among the modern London's playwrights back into Augustan Rome, calling Ovid and Virgil onstage to expound their respective theories of fame. More recently for Richardson, Alexander Pope had modernised Chaucer's *The House of Fame* (1379) – the most significant early introduction of the *fama* tradition into England – as *The Temple of Fame*, published in 1715. As Jeremy Tambling argues, English literature's early seizing on the structural similarity of fame and rumour in examples such as these indicates its wider preoccupation with 'the plurality of (the) circulation of messages' and 'the impossibility of any chronology establishing a single cause and effect'.[5] As much ideological store as it has set by ideas of fame and reputation, an awareness of the shakiness of fame's informational underpinnings, and the ease with which it can tumble into scurrilous rumour and rival retellings, has never been far away.

Late on in the novel, Clarissa attempts to circumvent the confusion of the two kinds of *fama*, proclaiming that 'as to the *world* and its *censures* … however desirous I always was of a fair fame, yet I never thought it right to give more than a *second place* to the world's opinion' (C 1139). When applied to a woman, 'fame' suggests sexual virtue or virginity, and Clarissa sometimes uses the word in this sense after Lovelace rapes her. In her mad papers written in the rape's immediate aftermath, Clarissa refers to Lovelace as a caterpillar who has destroyed 'the fair leaf of virgin fame' (C 892) and later thanks Anna for 'supporting my blighted fame against the busy tongues of uncharitable censurers' (C 1114). Clarissa wants fame in the sense of being beyond reproach sexually to be distinct from fame in the sense of being at the mercy of the 'busy tongues' of culture. The difficulty of making such a clear-cut division is in evidence from the very beginning of the novel.

Anna writes to Clarissa, having been confronted with rumours of the early dispute between Lovelace and Clarissa's brother and of Lovelace's romantic overtures to both Harlowe sisters. 'I know it must hurt you to become the subject of the public talk', Anna says, 'and yet upon an occasion so generally known it is impossible but that whatever relates to a young lady, whose distinguished merits have made her the public care, should engage everyone's attention' (C 39). Clarissa's merits have made her famous, but Anna sees how easily the sympathetic 'public care' this engenders can snap round into insidious rumour, or as Richardson has it here, 'public talk'. 'There are different reports', she continues, 'some people scrupling not to insinuate that the younger sister (at least by her uncommon merit) has stolen a lover from the elder' (C 40). As rumours are prone to do, this story doing the rounds that Clarissa has stolen her sister's lover recurs somewhat later in the novel, and with the new elaboration that Bella is still infatuated with Lovelace. This rumour, it turns out, has been started by Bella's servant Betty, who Bella – 'lay(ing) herself in the power of a servant's tongue! – Poor creature!' (C 85) – has been uncareful enough to confide in.

We have seen that earlier literary engagements with *fama* played on the difficulty of finding where rumours originate and 'the impossibility of any chronology' when it comes to how they subsequently spread. Anna, however, makes a surprisingly deft attempt at tracing how this particular rumour has come about:

> Betty (pleased to be thought worthy of a secret, and to have an opportunity of inveighing against Lovelace's perfidy, as she would have it to be) told it to one of *her* confidants; that confidant, with like injunctions of secrecy, to Miss Lloyd's Harriot – Harriot to Miss Lloyd – Miss Lloyd to *me* – I to you. (C 85)

Anna suggests that rumours are spread by each person only telling their most trusted confidante – each of whom trusts that the information would then go no further – in a process Anna tells us Lovelace has referred to as 'the *female round-about*'. In her study of gossip, Patricia Meyer Spacks addresses this common gendering of rumour and argues that as much as the term has been used as a way of dismissing female forms of conversation and sociability, gossip can also be defended as an important counterweight to the officially circumscribed public discourse.[6] There is little of this willingness to countenance a defence of rumour in Richardson's main female correspondents, however. Both Clarissa and Anna seem horrified by it, even when it is not directed at Clarissa. Weighing up Lovelace's attractiveness against his bad reputation, Anna decides that, even if the rumours about him are all untrue, he is still 'guilty of an inexcusable fault' in having allowed them to be spread about him at all. Lovelace's sin is the one Jonathan Swift has sometimes been accused of: 'pride in being thought worse than he is' (C 75).[7]

'Desirous', by contrast, 'of sliding through life to the end of it unnoted', Anna tells us that Clarissa has made '*rather useful than glaring*' her 'deserved motto' (C 40). When her family forbid her from attending church until she has consented to marry their preferred suitor, she recognises it as a means by which 'every ear (will) be opened against me; and every tale encouraged' (C 115), adding helplessly that 'my disgraces if they have to have an end, need not to be proclaimed to the whole world' (C 118). Clarissa continues to think in terms of how she is being represented at the level of public talk even at the most pivotal moments of the book's first instalment. When Clarissa first despondently considers allowing Lovelace to abduct her, she reflects that

> as to the world's opinion, it is impossible to imagine that the behaviour of my relations to me has not already brought upon my family those free censures they deserve ... I have no doubt that I am the talk, and perhaps the byword of half the country. If so, I am afraid I can now do nothing that will give me more disgrace. (C 349)

If this experience of having been brought low in public view momentarily emboldens Clarissa in her decision to flee with Lovelace, her panicked letter to Anna written on the other side of the escape continues to be expressed from the point of view of how it will be spoken about by others: 'you will soon hear (if already you have not heard from the mouth of common fame) that your Clarissa Harlowe is gone off with a man' (C 370).

Part of the trouble with rumours is that they are in at least one sense all true. The experience of getting to hear a rumour about oneself can be a disturbing combination of guilty recognition at what the rumour has got right and self-righteous outrage at what it's got wrong. In Shakespeare's *Twelfth Night*, Viola's brother, Sebastian, is mistaken by Sir Toby and Sir Andrew for Viola herself, who is at this point dressed as a man and looks identical to Sebastian. When the two knights challenge him, Sebastian beats them up, leading to a scene where Viola can only stand amazed at being accused of having done so. Encountering a rumour about oneself is like finding out we have some mysterious Sebastian-like double out there, living like us but doing things we don't recognise. Discussing the persistence of such cases of doubling in literature and film, Alenka Zupančič refers to them as fictions of the 'introduction of the Ego/I into what is called objective reality'.[8] We are used to thinking of 'what is on the inside' – our interior thoughts and convictions – as the defining thing about us, marking the limit of what psychoanalysts call our ego. Imagine our surprise, then, when we come up against evidence that far from being a mere abstraction within us, '*the ego exists*', as Zupančič puts it, and is just as 'out there' as Viola's double is. The truth of every rumour is that it 'exists' in this objective sense: on the plane of objective reality, being circulated among real people, affecting decisions they make and contributing to how our being is met with in the world. However untrue or inaccurate from the point of view of the person the rumour concerns, so long as the rumour is 'out there' having this kind of material effect on reality, it is a fundamental misunderstanding to think that we can keep some sort of true self haughtily separate from it.[9]

But between them at the start of the novel, Clarissa and Anna seem to be working towards just such a separation. Increasingly aware of the extent to which the rumours about Clarissa and her family are becoming entrenched as received notions, Richardson has them go as far as to make the meta-fictional gesture of calling on the form of the epistolary novel itself as a kind of counter-discourse, preserving Clarissa's account of herself against the manipulations of the culture of rumour around her. The first letter shows Anna inviting Clarissa to undercut this mess of rumour by writing 'the whole of your story', in the hope that 'your account of all things previous to it will be your justification' (C 40). As William Beatty Warner puts it, what Anna has in mind is 'a story that carries its own meaning, a story that is sufficiently convincing in its method of narration as to obviate any need for our interpretation'.[10] Richardson himself seems to share Anna's initial faith in the potential Clarissa's account has to provide an ideal counter-discourse to the other malformed and conflicting rival accounts developing at the novel's margins. In the early phase of the Harlowes' suspicions about Clarissa's relationship with Lovelace, Clarissa submits the letters they have exchanged to her mother, who reports back that she has 'nothing to task your discretion with' (C 100). Even at the very end of the long period of his creative tinkering with the text, Richardson added another version of this scene to the conclusion to the novel's third edition, showing Clarissa's parents once again reading her letters and conceding that their daughter had been innocent all along (3C VIII, 252).

Richardson's belief that epistolary writing can somehow overcome the manipulations of rumour is supported by the eighteenth-century truism that letters are to be prized for the unmediated access they supposedly give to the hearts of the letter-writers. In a well-known letter to his friend Sarah Wescomb, Richardson goes as far as to propose that letter-writing might even be more intimate than actually being in the company of the person you write to. 'Who', he asks,

> shall decline the converse of the pen? the pen that makes distance, presence; and brings back to sweet remembrance all the delights of presence; which makes even presence but body while absence becomes the soul; and leaves no room for the intrusion of breakfast-calls, or dinner or supper directions, which often broke in upon us.[11]

For Jacques Derrida, writing has historically tended to be treated as a grudgingly tolerated supplement, resorted to only when separation makes properly present speech impossible.[12] By contrast, letter-writing for Richardson is not only just as present as actually being in the room but in fact is even more present because it is communication enacted in a state of full focus, without the humdrum interruptions and distractions that too often characterise conversation in person.

The first problem with this opposition between the colliding manipulations of rumour and the unmediated openness of the epistolary form, however, is that an epistolary novel is uniquely ill placed to claim to be an unmediated anything. This is because it is, in a certain sense, *all media*. The many memorable instances in the history of letter-writing where the transcendent 'message' of the letter has failed to rise above or has ended up being secondary to the material object of the letter itself attest to this. As the psychoanalyst Darian Leader argues, the moment in James Joyce's love letters to his wife, Nora, where he moves from graphically describing sexual acts to asking her to masturbate using the letter itself should remind us that there 'at least two functions of the letter: as a message and as an object'.[13] Thomas O. Beebee discusses an anecdote from the 1940s that lends itself to a similar reading. A German woman whose husband was away in the war became fixated on anonymously sending obscene letters to the people in her village. The identities of the recipients, it seems, was completely unimportant to her, but the act of sending the mere object of the letter itself lent itself to supreme sexual enjoyment.[14] As Jacques Lacan points out in his analysis of Edgar Allen Poe's story, 'The Purloined Letter', a letter is never merely a message expiring on delivery but rather is an object that goes on delivering, as if with a life of its own: 'if we could say that a letter has fulfilled its destiny after having served its function, the ceremony of returning letters would be a less commonly accepted way to bring to a close the extinguishing of the fires of Cupid's festivities'.[15]

Alternatively, the content or 'message' part of a letter also has a curious propensity to switch sides, becoming 'objectified' in a similar way once it has left our hands. The tragicomic figure (portrayed for one by Rik Mayall in an episode of the British sitcom *Bottom*) of the lonely man who sends birthday cards and Valentine messages to himself and responds gleefully when they arrive is one example. A notorious tragic variation presented itself in 2013 when a British teenager killed herself after suffering an anonymous campaign of bullying messages online. On investigating, the managers of the website the tormentors had apparently used to send the messages made the extraordinary claim that the majority of them had been posted from the girl's own computer. Assuming this to be true, it is as if she could only carry out the suicide once the necessary objects of the in-part-imagined online hate campaign had been laid out around her: even if this meant momentarily disavowing the fact that she was herself the original sender. Once again, the letter as 'message' had been relegated to the status of the letter as 'object', no longer a direct articulation of subjectivity but an object that we may encounter 'out there' on the plane of objective reality.

We will see that this objectness of the letter – its propensity to assert itself as an object beyond the message we intended it to convey – is something that Richardson becomes increasingly preoccupied with as *Clarissa* develops. One effect of this is to draw attention to the way in which Richardson's great claim in *Clarissa*'s preface that its letters 'abound not only with critical situations, but with what may be called instantaneous descriptions and reflections' (C 35) is simultaneously true and false. Unlike most other kinds of continuous first- or third-person narration, the principal narrative voices in epistolary novels are indeed produced in a constantly renewed state of ignorance as to how the events they record in a given moment are going to transpire. And this lends itself to sustaining a particular strain of anxiety, which it wasn't especially within, say, Daniel Defoe's power to create. But at the same time, for Richardson to call the little capsule narratives of his individual letters 'instantaneous' is putting it strongly, since the one thing that can be said of a letter is that it has always by necessity already missed the 'instant' it narrates: it can only ever be a belated representation of something that, however recently, has already passed. In this respect, a better way of visualising the form might be to think of the enormous collection of interlocking half-open matchboxes Lacan once said he had seen arranged around the house of the poet Jacques Prévert.[16] In a manner resembling those little slotted-together sleeves and trays, while a given letter in *Clarissa* is being written, the events that will be recorded in the next are already passing away.

Rumours are Richardson's first example of how chance ideas can ossify into reality and become enshrined and received as truth. Clarissa and Anna begin the novel with some faith that their own epistolary correspondence can provide some sort of resistance to such received notions, but this ignores the extent to which the letters too are necessarily subject to a manipulable and mediated circulation of messages. What is more, the opposition also elides how dangerously similar the circulation of epistolary correspondence is to that which goes on in rumour and the extent to which the reader they most need to convince – the real-life reader of Richardson's novels – is placed by necessity on the side of that rumour-mongering public peeking in.

To demonstrate this with one final comparison: John Locke took the question of epistolary writing's suitedness to unmediated communication in yet another direction in the preface to his *Paraphrase* of the epistles of Saint Paul in 1707. Locke warns of the vulnerability of Paul's writings to heterodox interpretation, particularly if the reader overlooks the fact that

> the nature of epistolary writings in general, disposes the writer to pass by the mentioning of many things, as well known to him to whom his letter is address'd, which are necessary to be laid open to a stranger, to make him comprehend what is said: and it not seldom falls out, that a well penn'd letter which is very easy and intelligible to the receiver, is very obscure to a stranger, who hardly knows what to make of it.[17]

The very qualities that make letters so intuitively comprehensible to their intended recipients can render them almost unreadable to everyone else. While Locke and Richardson's contemporaries were very comfortable with the literary epistle as a genre of formal public address used by scientists, lawyers and philosophers alike, Locke quite audaciously returns Paul's contribution to the genre to the historically specific correspondence between persons it originated in. For Locke, the obscure parts in Paul do not indicate inconsistencies in doctrine but simply mark moments when we readers are not in on the culturally specific details Paul assumed he could 'pass by the mentioning of' when addressing the recipient at hand.

For all Richardson's claims for the transparent immediacy of epistolary communication, he lets slip a similar awareness of this problem underlying all published correspondence – fictional or otherwise – in *Clarissa*'s first letter. The 'whole ... story' Anna hopes will break with the haphazard constructions of rumour might take its authority from Clarissa and Anna's own idealised and ideally candid 'converse of the pen', but to replicate anything like this transparency of meaning for the novel's real-life readers, it has to avoid the kinds of familiar contraction and unglossed local specificity that in Locke's view made Paul's epistles so difficult to read. Richardson's way around this is to have Anna ask Clarissa to 'write in so full a manner as may gratify those who know not so much of your affairs as I do' (C 40): which is to say, envisage me as your interlocutor but also the as-yet-unknown public who may one day read our letters. If Anna's request looks forward to the way Clarissa will later try to justify herself to her family by revealing her letters, it also represents a surreptitious concession to the real-life reader, positioned as she is on the side of the uninformed public looking in on the private world of the correspondents.

II

Formed in a circulation of disembodied missives and betraying a dim awareness of the fact that it is the fate of their intimate exchanges to be 'made public', epistolary novels end up having a fair bit in common with the rumours that so often work their way through their fictional worlds. But so too rumour and the received notions it threatens to reinforce are shadily implicated in the other literary form that Richardson worked his novels into: the anthology of sententious maxims. As we have seen, in 1753 and 1755, Richardson compiled two versions of a *Collection of Moral Sentiments* sourced from *Clarissa* and then from his other novels, perhaps in a last attempt to lay down the law on his texts' moral content in a way that the open-ended ambiguity of his novels had never really allowed.

In *Sententiousness and the Novel* (1985), Geoffrey Bennington has examined the pithy generalisations and epigrammatic phrases that stud the fictions of Richardson's contemporaries as well as the strange appearance of wisdom and authority they seem to imbue them with. Something of this appearance of authority comes from the fact that such 'propositions stand out from their context and seem to invite extraction: they can quite happily be read in isolation from their surroundings'. For Bennington, this gives them a paradoxical place as far as the authority of the text is concerned. The fact that they retain their power even when taken outside the running of the source text grants them the authority to speak loftily on its behalf: Richardson's initial representation of the maxims in the *Collection*s as the true core of the wisdom of his novels is consistent with this view, for one. But at the same time, the separability of such maxims also undercuts that authority because statements that are not so entangled in the text proper that they can't still be understood outside, were presumably not all that essential to it in the first place. 'Maxims in texts are thus substantial and excessive, the best of the text and the rest of the text', Bennington concludes, with anthologies of such maxims merely serving to 'gather up and monumentalise inscriptions now made lapidary: "the rest" in peace'.[18]

Richardson himself came to regret the 'dry performance' of the *Collection*, dismissing its maxims as so much 'dull morality ... divested of story'.[19] And yet, as Bennington warns, such phrases already imply their own removal, even before the anthologist arrives and this divesting of story occurs. If the

Collection had never been conceived, Richardson's sententious maxims would still have the status of zombie phrases stumbling around his texts, simultaneously mystically powerful and dead on arrival.[20] But if Richardson seems only partially aware of these complications within his own didactic use of sententious phrases, his representation of their use by characters within *Clarissa* itself is considerably more nuanced. Received notions gather and confirm themselves in the culture of public talk just outside the novel's main cast, but they are equally important to the even more directly pernicious establishment of dubious truths among Clarissa's immediate family themselves. After her refusal to marry Solmes, Clarissa tells Anna that 'my assembled relations have taken an *unanimous* resolution ... against me' (C 217). This unanimity, so important to the novel's plot because it is what drives Clarissa to briefly open herself up to the possibility of absconding with Lovelace, is the direct result of a process of quotation and reiteration of certain phrases within the family, which elevates them to the status of deployable maxims embodying received notions.

That families can establish a sense of unanimity by means of the repetition of certain stock phrases would come as no surprise to an aristocratic one like Lovelace's. At an early point in the novel when his standing with the Harlowes is relatively good, we hear for instance how Lovelace's personal generosity is undergirded by such familial mottos: 'it was a maxim with his family, from which he would by no means depart, never to rack-rent old tenants or their descendants' (C 78–9). Elsewhere, Lovelace writes about himself in terms of heraldic mottos supposedly guiding and embodying his character and behaviour: the Virgilian *debellare superbos* (overthrow the proud) 'should be my motto, were I to have a new one' (C 162). And later he imagines a future family portrait with Clarissa, inscribed with the motto 'IN COELO SALUS – or QUIE perhaps' ('in heaven salvation ... or rest'), 'if they have happened to live the usual married life of brawl and contradiction' (C 970).[21]

The Harlowes may have no such well-heeled relationship to mottos and the family traditions they instate, but they do use figures of speech of one kind or another a great deal. Clarissa's brother James's irritation at Clarissa's special treatment in their grandfather's will is made worse by the fact that he has apparently had 'often in his mouth' the 'familiar and low expression ... "That a man who has sons brings up chickens for his own table ... whereas daughters are chickens brought up for the tables of other men"' (C 77). In the same letter, Clarissa refers to her sister's 'old saw' – used here to defend marrying Clarissa off to the landed Solmes – that '*it is good to be related to an estate*' (C 81). And when Clarissa politely asks after Solmes during a subsequent meeting of the family, Bella intones with similar worldly wise sententiousness, '*Proud spirits may be brought to*' (C 88). This habit of using proverbial-sounding phrases extends to the family's servants and to Clarissa herself, as in the unusually affable episode in which Clarissa exchanges 'proverb for proverb' (C 263) with Betty during one of their arguments. So far, the maxims we have noted are not very different to those used in Richardson's more satirical portrayals of pseudo-wisdom, such as Lovelace's uncle Lord M or the scholarly pedant Elias Brand, but early in the novel's first instalment, an important shift in the Harlowes' use of them occurs. As part of their programme of what Castle calls 'linguistic persecution', the Harlowes start applying the detachable logic of maxims not just to traditional mottos and everyday proverbs but simply to ordinary phrases that the family members have used, so elevating them to the status of received wisdom to be deployed against Clarissa.

Clarissa may exhibit a certain horror of the grass-roots chatter of rumour, but it does at least sometimes back up her position. When her family tries to force her to marry Solmes, she finds that in the public talk, 'every mouth is opened against him for his sordid ways' (C 101). Things are very different within the Harlowe household however. There, by contrast,

> the *generous* Mr Solmes is now his character! ... He is accordingly, in every visit he makes, not only highly caressed by the principals of our family, but obsequiously attended and

cringed to by the menials – and *the noble settlements* are echoed from every mouth.

Noble is the word used to enforce the offers of a man who is mean enough to *hate*. (C 81)

If rumours and sententious proverbs both show that you can make something seem true if you say it enough times, the Harlowes play the same trick in the language they join in using repeatedly about Solmes, refiguring his character flaws into virtues. In the same letter, Clarissa slips into italics when mimicking her family's commandments, which are evidently becoming ubiquitous enough to be unattributable to any one person specifically: 'I ... *am to be as dependent upon my papa's will as a daughter ought to be who knows not what is good for herself.* This is the language of the family now' (C 80).

Something of the workings of this weirdly spectral family language being 'echoed from every mouth' can be glimpsed in Letter 32.4: Clarissa's Uncle Antony's reply to one of her letters appealing to him for sympathy. Like the other family members, Antony begins by using conventional phrases to talk down Clarissa's arguments. Solomon's admonition, '*he that is first in his own cause ... seemeth just: but his neighbour cometh and searcheth him*' (C 154), and the traditional proverb 'what's *sauce for the goose is sauce for the gander*' (C 157) are dropped into his letter to warn Clarissa that her version of events is not going to win out over those of her family and that the outspokenness of her letters petitioning them is being taken as a licence for them to respond in kind: 'it behoves US not to speak in'. Turning to Clarissa's complaints about Solmes' inadequate literacy, however, Antony reaches not for Scripture or the common stock of folk wisdom for a reference, but to Clarissa's own brother: 'I am absolutely of your brother's mind, that reading and writing, though not too much for the wits of you young girls, are too much for your judgements' (C 155). The worry that literacy might prove too much for female sanity is a familiar one in the discourse surrounding the novel in the period: but here the parallelism of James Harlowe-via-Antony's phrasing lends it a special appearance of balanced, reasoned authority as well the kind of epigrammatic detachability Bennington describes.[22] In other words, in the instant of quotation, James's familiar misogynistic grumbling becomes magically elevated to the same high status of Antony's other on-hand authorities. Antony follows this by doing the same for Clarissa's father, citing 'your good father's maxim', '*Too ready forgiveness does but encourage offences*', and adding that 'there would not be so many headstrong daughters as there are, if this maxim were kept in mind' (C 156). Part of what is disturbing about this is how incestuously self-confirming these acts of quotation are, as the unremarkable prejudices of one family member congeal and solidify into generally applicable authorities when they reappear under the pen of another. The authority of both the person quoting and the person being quoted seems to spring spontaneously and simultaneously from this performative act of citation.

The significance of Antony's citation of Clarissa's father's maxim is compounded in the awkward afterlife Richardson grants the phrase '*Too ready forgiveness does but encourage offences*' in the *Collection of Moral Sentiments*. Something a little like the conception of forgiveness paraded by Clarissa's father and uncle – that it should be withheld from Clarissa for her own good – will return in a massively more dramatic form in the late part of the novel when, in the face of all pressure to the contrary, Clarissa refuses to forgive Lovelace after the rape. As I will argue in Chapter 3, Clarissa's refusal to forgive at this point is part of her general tragic refusal to sacrifice her desire to the will of those around her, the importance of which is absolutely structural to the tragic pattern of the novel. To connect the upper reaches of the novel's tragic pattern with something as banal as the ageing bachelor Antony's views on bringing up teenage girls may seem peculiar, but that is effectively what Richardson does in the apparatus of the 1755 version of the *Collection*. In the section headed 'Forgiveness', the maxim shared between Clarissa's uncle and father becomes a statement not about Clarissa but about Lovelace, rewritten as 'MANY a young offender against modesty and decency has been confirmed a libertine by too easy forgiveness' (CL 124). The *Collection* refers any reader curious about seeing the passage in context to Letters 187.1–4, which in the original novel are a strung together series of passages from Lovelace and Belford written around the time of Clarissa's imprisonment with Lovelace before the rape. But turning to these passages the reader looks in vain for anything like the maxim as it is quoted in the *Collection*. Instead, the closest thing to it is Lovelace's description of how inhibited he feels in the face of Clarissa's rather eerie and unblinking virtue: something which, he says, 'never before, no not in my first attempt, young as I then was, and frighted at my own boldness (till I found myself *forgiven*), had such an effect upon me!' (C 602).

This first lover who let slide the boldness of Lovelace's early advances thereby 'confirmed a libertine'. The passage may not actually contain the maxim about 'too ready forgiveness' as it appears in the *Collection*, but the maxim works very effectively as a judgement upon it. It would have been better not to forgive him at all, the *Collection* belatedly suggests, and Clarissa, as we later see, will not make the same mistake. For Richardson then, the maxim was wrong when Antony quoted James Harlowe using it against Clarissa but mysteriously becomes right when the *Collection* starts inviting us to use it against Lovelace. The twitchy way these received notions have of leaping into other contexts in order to confirm themselves goes even beyond the actions of the characters in the novel, into Richardson's own treatment of the text after it had been published.

So far, we have seen how the Harlowes set the logic of the received notion against Clarissa, employing the authority of maxims and proverbs and even elevating each other's own utterances to the same kind of mystical authority. But, yet more troublingly, they treat Clarissa's own statements with the same kind of detachability. In Letter 16, Clarissa's emotional refusal to marry Solmes is interpreted by her mother and sister as evidence of her dangerous attachment to Lovelace. When they confront her with this, Clarissa replies:

> I declare to you that I know not my own heart if it be not absolutely free. And pray, let me ask, my dearest mamma, in what has my conduct been faulty that, like a giddy creature, I must be forced to marry, to save me from – from what? Let me beseech you, madam, to be the guardian of my reputation – Let not your Clarissa be precipitated into a state she wishes not to enter into with any man! (C 90–1)

This is written slightly after Anna's letter asking whether Lovelace might just prompt an unusual 'throb, throb, throb' (C 71) in Clarissa's heart and Clarissa's protest that even on being told of Lovelace's admirable acts of generosity, 'I had no *throbs*, no *glows* upon it' (C 79). It is possible to detect a masterful bit of equivocation in Clarissa's claim to 'know not my own heart if it be not absolutely free', since it could be reasonably rephrased as *I permit myself to desire Lovelace provided I'm not consciously aware of it*. In this way, one can imagine the passage being employed to give support to the long-standing interpretation of the novel that sees it in terms of Clarissa's secret desire for Lovelace.[23] All in all, the persistence of that reading is troubling, creepily repeating as it does the Harlowes' prurient speculations on Clarissa's desire, or, still worse, the 'she wants it really' attitude of Lovelace.[24] But even putting this aside, the significance of Clarissa's claim that her 'heart is free' is less in the question of the truthfulness of the claim than in what Richardson shows happening to it afterwards.

Clarissa's mother begins to reply to Clarissa using Clarissa's own phrase, 'if your heart be free –' before being interrupted by further argument from her daughter. After this, Mrs Harlowe finally gets round to using Clarissa's words sardonically against her 'I will come up to you again. See that I find you as I wish to find you, and since *your heart is free*, let your duty govern it' (C 91). This repetition sets in motion a tendency that will resound over the next forty or so letters, wherein the Harlowes' technique of granting their own statements the authority of sententious proverbs becomes applied in reverse to Clarissa's claims about herself, in order to erode their plausibility. Clarissa describes her mother bringing up the argument again in the following letter. Mrs Harlowe is evidently taken with Clarissa's phrase 'my heart is free', repeating it four times in the long argument that ensues. Abstracted from the context in which Clarissa actually said it, the phrase has become remodelled into evidence that she is in a position to accept Solmes: 'you declare that *your heart is free* … I rejoice in the hope that you are convinced. This indeed seems to be a proof of the welcome truth you have asserted, that *your heart is free*' (C 96–7). This logical slippage established, Mrs Harlowe seizes on the supposed inconsistency of the claim with Clarissa's refusal to marry him as proof that she must be lying: 'your heart *free*! Clarissa! How can you tell me your heart is free? Such extraordinary antipathies to a particular person must be owing to extraordinary prepossessions in another's favour' (C 98).

A few letters later, we find Mrs Harlowe still using the phrase: a repetitiveness Clarissa acknowledges when she says, 'I had owned (the old string!) *that my heart was free*' (C 110). By now however, in a version of the pattern we saw in Uncle Antony's quotations from Clarissa's father and brother, Mrs Harlowe attributes the ongoing use of the phrase to Clarissa's father: 'he had declared, he had rather have no daughter in me, than one he could not dispose of for her own good: especially as I had owned, that my *heart was free*; and as the general good of his whole family was to be promoted by my obedience' (C 109). In this way, Clarissa's passing remark has been entered into 'the language of the family', virtually reversing its meaning to become part of the pattern of received notions that the Harlowes reinforce between them. Clarissa acknowledges the trap she has fallen into when she reflects that her family 'have grounded their principal argument for my compliance with their will upon my acknowledgements that my heart is free' (C 136) and that 'the declaration that my heart was *free* afforded them an argument to prove obstinacy and perverseness upon me, since it could be nothing else that governed me in my opposition to their wills' (C 176). By Letter 50, the structuring of 'the language of the family' around a single statement of Clarissa's has become cemented in a series of letters from her brother James that cite the phrase a further three times, by now in aggressively derisive mode: 'your heart is *free* you know – It *must* – For, did you not tell your mother it was? And will the *pious* Clarissa Harlowe fib to her mamma?' (C 224, also 218, 223).

As was the case with the maxim about 'too ready forgiveness', there is a strange coda to this violent detachment and afterlife of this quotation from Clarissa's argument with her mother. In Letter 174, written a month into her long internment with Lovelace, Clarissa speculates on the possibility that either Anna's suitor, Mr Hickman, or the ladies in Lovelace's family may be able to intervene to relieve her dreadful situation, which she acknowledges was brought about by her initial error in judgement in first trusting Lovelace. She thinks of the 1679 version of the Oedipus story by John Dryden and Nathaniel Lee, a play she will cling to once more in the mad fragments she composes after the rape. 'It were an impiety to adopt the following lines', she cautions, 'because it would be throwing upon the decrees of Providence a fault too much my own. But often do I revolve them, for the sake of the general similitude which they bear to my unhappy yet undesigned error' (C 568). In Dryden and Lee's play, the passage Clarissa quotes appears at the end of Act III, following Tiresius' accusation that Oedipus himself is the cause of the plague at Thebes as a result of his unwitting parricide and incest. Waiting for the arrival of a retired servant who reportedly witnessed the killing of King Laius, and so is the only person who can corroborate Tiresius' vision, Oedipus reflects on how in this instant he is precariously poised between guilt and innocence, in a situation where for the time being both past and future are radically unknowable.

This is the passage as Clarissa cites it:

> To you, great gods! I make my last appeal:
> Or clear my virtues, or my crimes reveal.
> If wand'ring in the maze of life I run,
> And backward tread the steps I sought to shun,
> Impute my errors to your own decree;
> My FEET are guilty; but my HEART is free.
>
> (III.i.587–93)[25]

The misquotation of 'feet' for Dryden and Lee's 'hands' in the last line brings the passage closer to the nature of Clarissa's crime: that of, as she puts it, having 'gone off with a man' (C 370), as well the passage's own internal imagery of wandering, running and stepping. Yet more adventurously, the misquotation also pulls the passage into line with a plot detail in the Oedipus story. His name meaning 'swollen footed', Oedipus' damaged feet are, until the servant's arrival at least, both the most physically manifest and the most disavowed piece of evidence for his guilt, having waited as evidence throughout a long sexual relationship between him and Jocasta. As Jocasta recalls, in order to avoid the prediction that their child would grow up to be Laius' murderer, 'the wretched infant of a guilty fate' was 'bor'd through his untry'd feet, and bound with cords / on a bleak mountain, naked was exposed' (III.i.509–11).

Clarissa's meditation on this passage at a point in the novel when the outcome of her own transgression has become static, seemingly irresolvably deferred, is significant for the early association it makes between Clarissa herself and the heroes of tragedy. The episode was one that stuck in Fielding's mind too: in *Joseph Andrews* (1742) he compares Joseph and Fanny's trepidation on discovering they might be brother and sister to Oedipus' wait in this part of the myth.[26] But, perhaps more importantly, Clarissa's quotation materially alters the significance of the phrase 'my heart is free' that had taken on such power in the Harlowes' aggressive repetition of it after Clarissa's earlier self-defence. Thus far, we have treated that key phrase as if it originated from Clarissa, only to be thrown into multiple manipulative applications in the vindictive citations of the Harlowes. But suddenly we run into a problem. If Dryden and Lee's lines are familiar enough for Clarissa to 'often … revolve them' at this later point, then presumably they were already so when she first uttered a variation on them in the argument with her mother just over two months before. In this small slippage, the insight emerges that in the world of *Clarissa* there is no original utterance prior to the repetitions of rumour, sententious maxims and malicious quotations. Just as the epistolary form cannot convincingly distinguish itself from the manipulations of rumour, Clarissa's supposedly free statements about herself are themselves already determined by the logic of the received notion. It will take more than a return to 'the original' to break out of its grasp.

III

I began this chapter by suggesting that the dangerous spreading of received notions Richardson mentions in the preface becomes one of the more material forms of 'linguistic persecution' enacted against Clarissa in the first instalment. Claims about Clarissa are allowed to pass as fact among the wider public beyond the novel's letter-writing characters and internally among the Harlowes, apparently only on the basis that the more an idea is repeated the greater the appearance of truthfulness it takes on. As we will see presently, Richardson's major retort to this dimension of public talk comes in the form of tragedy. But before moving to this, it is worth noting that Lovelace too is by no means free from the logic of the received notion.

Lovelace claims to dislike proverbs and ridicules his uncle Lord M's compulsive use of them:

> when a boy, I never asked anything of him, but out flew a proverb ... this gave me so great an aversion to the very word, that when a child, I made it a condition with my tutor, who was an honest parson, that I would not read my Bible at all, if he would not excuse me one of the wisest books in it: to which, however, I had no other objection than that it was called *The Proverbs*. (C 610–11)

However, this does not prevent him from employing a certain proverbial logic in his own writing and behaviour. Readers have long noted that Lovelace is one for slightly slapdash illustrative quotations, 'some drawn from historical sources, some made up on the spot ... to lend hokey "authority" to his interpretation of events', or otherwise 'like ... an educated man who feels free to do as he pleases with the resources at his command simply for the occasion, and assuming that his audience can supply the original in its proper context'.[27] But yet more fundamentally Richardson represents libertinism itself as determined by the authority-instituting logic of the received notion or maxim.

When he writes of his own libertinism, Lovelace advocates a kind of free love, practised in natural and unfettered spontaneity: 'Could a man do as the birds do, change every Valentine's day (a *natural* appointment! for birds have not the *sense*, forsooth, to fetter themselves, as we wiseacre men take great and solemn pains to do)' (C 872). But libertinism in Richardson's novels is not usually represented as a matter of spontaneous instinct. When, in *Sir Charles Grandison*, Harriet Byron's suitor Mr Greville complains that Harriet thinks 'that I am a libertine; that we have all one dialect; and that I can say nothing new, or that is worthy of your attention' (SCG I, 104), he signals the way in which libertinism can be seen less as an expression of freewheeling liberty than as its own system of structured norms: a shared subcultural 'dialect' founded on a common stock of what Lovelace himself refers to as a 'libertine's creed' (C 633) of 'rakish maxims' (C 930).

An example of this in action appears in Frances Sheridan's *Memoirs of Miss Sidney Bidulph*, published with a dedication to Richardson in 1761, in which the heroine's brother defends her rakish fiancé when he is exposed for having made a former lover pregnant: 'He would make a merit of having formed no designs upon the young lady; why possibly, he did not, till he found the poor soul was so smitten with him … a man *must* not reject a lady upon these occasions'.[28] The justification appeals to a kind of parodic system of etiquette that makes libertinism into a matter of propriety and good manners in itself. It is the logic of Lady Booby in *Joseph Andrews*, who thinks that once she has overcome her own sexual scruples and propositioned Joseph it is an act of impertinence for him to retain his own by refusing her.[29] If a woman is smitten enough with a man to be seduced by him, then doing so is not so much a momentarily uncontrolled lapse in morals as an important social obligation. This version of libertinism falls somewhere between, on the one hand, the kind of thing that had previously been said about fashion, and, on the other, what the nineteenth century called 'good form', which, for men at least, included among its meanings being decent enough to know when to depart slightly from what is strictly moral. *Much Ado about Nothing*'s reference to fashion as a 'deformed thief' (III. iii.120) remorselessly ruining its followers by constantly changing its historical grab bag of styles gets smartened up in the Restoration in *The Man of Mode*'s jokes about the fashion victim being 'beholding to his education for making him so eminent a coxcomb' (I.i.393–4).[30] In *The Beggar's Opera*, this formula of saying something outrageous or ostensibly undesirable in the manner of a wise moral rule underlies the comedy of Gay's parody petit-bourgeois couple, the Peachums, who in Act I are as outraged that their daughter has risked her fortune and prospects by actually marrying her lover as a real petit-bourgeois couple would be if she hadn't.[31]

Richardson may have been just the kind of person at whom Gay's joke was aimed, but he also couldn't have been naive to its structure. Faced with the uproar that he meets with after the rape, Lovelace asks Belford with only partly mock ingenuousness, 'what have I done more than prosecute the maxims by which thou and I and every rake are governed?' (C 970). As Lacan argues in the more extreme setting of his essay 'Kant with Sade', at the level of structure there is not much difference between the compulsion of the moral law and the compulsion to transgress it.[32] One thinks of today's culture of 'pickup artists' who train hapless geeks in the art of seduction using a tyrannically managed programme of lectures, workshops and rehearsed anecdotes and chat-up lines. The libertine maxim of this kind most commonly discussed in *Clarissa* is '*once subdued, always subdued*', a contraction of the idea that once a woman has been either seduced or raped she will no longer care about her virtue and will consent to all subsequent sexual advances. Relating the elaborate story of one of the few adulteries he says he has been involved in, for example, Lovelace says that having tricked the woman into sleeping with him, 'the ice once broken (*once subdued, always subdued*)', she 'co-operated' thereafter (C 675).

'*Once subdued, always subdued*' is employed again and again in Lovelace's attempt to orchestrate the seduction of Clarissa and ends up being included in the *Collection of Moral Sentiments* under the heading 'Libertine, Rake', on the basis, Richardson says, that the reader needs to be able to identify it as 'an article in the Rake's Creed' (CL 149). Suggestively enough, it also represents a kind of libertine reversal of the received notion Richardson emphasises in the preface – 'reformed rakes make the best husbands' – as Lovelace himself suggests when he rephrases it as 'coy maids made fond wives' (C 238). Katherine Binhammer has argued that the phrase '*once subdued, always subdued*' reveals Lovelace's 'sense of how the events of seduction are sequenced', as if every seduction proceeded by the same inevitable series of stages, and, when it comes to women's behaviour, one could already 'see the end in the beginning'.[33] This imagined ability to collapse whole narratives into a simple maxim has evidently long been part of Lovelace's seduction programme. 'I have tried a young creature by a bad book, a light quotation, or an indecent picture', he says, 'and if she has borne that, or only blushed … that girl have I … put down for our own' (C 521).

The libertine women at Mrs Sinclair's share this analysis of the temporality of seduction, even looking back on their own biographies as evidence for it. When Lovelace expresses reluctance to rape Clarissa, he finds it is the women around him who most press him to do so: 'Sally and Polly upbraidingly remind me of my first attempts upon themselves – Yet force answers not my end – And yet it may, if there be truth in that part of the libertine's creed, *that once subdued, is always subdued*. And what woman answers *affirmatively* to the question?' (C 633–4). As much as 'the libertine's creed', the women themselves stand as sort of living maxims, testament to the reliability of a stock narrative they have already fulfilled and assume that Clarissa is also predisposed to. Assuring him later of 'the inclinations and hypocrisy of the whole sex', Sally even mockingly assures Lovelace that once Clarissa marries him, 'some other person would not find half the difficulty that [he] had found' (C 940–1). Rape, in this analysis, is always justified and forgiven in retrospect when the woman turns libertine herself. Indeed, if no woman ever actually 'answers affirmatively' and consents to sex, then rape, in a horrifying exaggeration of the kinds of inverted morality we have seen in *The Beggar's Opera* and elsewhere, becomes a grim kind of social obligation.

In this way, the self-confirming logic of the received notion and the 'linguistic persecution' it threatens is found in *Clarissa* on all sides. But the fate of the phrase '*once subdued, always subdued*' is also indicative of what the novel has in store for the apparently unavoidable dominance of the received notions later on. Struggling to understand Clarissa's outright refusal of his attempts to make amends and his offer to marry her after the rape, Lovelace declaims to Belford: 'before I knew this lady, we have pursued from pretty girl to pretty girl, as fast as we had set one down, taking another up – just as the fellows do with their flying-coaches and flying-horses at a country fair – with a *Who rides next! Who rides next!*' (C 970). The dependable rhythm of a fairground ride meets with an unbridgeable interruption which Lovelace makes quite clear is to be located in the unprecedented and violent splendour of Clarissa herself. 'Who would have thought there had been such a woman in the world?', Lovelace asks: 'of all the sex I have hitherto known, or heard, or read of, it was *once subdued, and always subdued*. The first struggle was generally the last' (C 904). As Lovelace admits a little later, 'this dear girl gives the lie to all our rakish maxims ... *Once subdued, always subdued* – 'Tis an egregious falsehood! – But oh, Jack, she never *was subdued*' (C 930). And then again, 'for the *fiftieth* time ... let me ask thee, who would have thought that there had been such a woman in the world?' (C 936).

In this chapter I have aimed to substantiate my claim that the reference to the 'received notion' in Richardson's preface is not just a passing moralistic afterthought but a constituent priority of the entire novel. We have seen that a stock of repeated phrases and maxims is at the heart of all of the kinds of discursive authority introduced in the novel prior to the rape: whether in the machinations of public talk, the Harlowes' construction of their case against Clarissa or the shared language of Lovelace and the libertines. As we will see, however, the fate of '*once subdued, always subdued*' – and Lovelace's amazement at its complete failure to account for the behaviour of Clarissa – is representative of a thoroughgoing collapse of the received notion once the novel enters its tragic phase.

Notes

1. For recent comment on the well-known tale of *Pamela*'s provincial reception, see Thomas Keymer and Peter Sabor, *Pamela the Marketplace: Literary Controversy and Print Culture in Eighteenth-Century Britain and Ireland* (Cambridge: Cambridge University Press, 2005), pp. 39–40; and Kate Loveman, *Reading Fictions, 1660–1740: Deception in English Literary and Political Culture* (Farnham: Ashgate, 2008), pp. 183–4.
2. Samuel Richardson, *Correspondence with Aaron Hill and the Hill Family*, ed. Christine Gerrard (Cambridge: Cambridge University Press, 2013), p. 259.
3. Terry Castle, *Clarissa's Ciphers: Meaning and Disruption in Richardson's Clarissa* (Ithaca: Cornell University Press, 1982), pp. 89, 59.
4. Philip Hardie, *Rumour and Renown: Representations of Fama in Western Literature* (Cambridge: Cambridge University Press, 2012), p. 3.
5. Jeremy Tambling, *On Anachronism* (Manchester: Manchester University Press, 2010), p. 69.
6. Patricia Meyer Spacks, *Gossip* (New York: Knopf, 1985), pp. 38–42.
7. See Leo Damrosch, *Jonathan Swift: His Life and His World* (New Haven, Conn.: Yale University Press, 2013), p. 6.
8. Alenka Zupančič, *The Odd One In: On Comedy* (Cambridge, Mass.: The MIT Press, 2008), p. 73.
9. Another version of my argument here appears in EDA Collective, *Twerking to Turking: Everyday Analysis, volume 2*, ed. Alfie Bown and Daniel Bristow (Alresford: Zero Books, 2015), pp. 237–8.
10. William Warner, *Reading Clarissa: The Struggles of Interpretation* (New Haven, Conn.: Yale University Press, 1979), p. 6.
11. Samuel Richardson, *Correspondence with Sarah Wescomb, Frances Grainger and Laetitia Pilkington*, ed. John Dussinger (Cambridge: Cambridge University Press, 2015), p. 7.

12 Jacques Derrida, *Of Grammatology*, trans. Gayatri Chakravorty Spivak (Baltimore, Md.: Johns Hopkins University Press, 1997).
13 Darian Leader, *Why Do Women Write More Letters Than They Post?* (London: Faber & Faber, 1997), p. 124.
14 Thomas O. Beebee, *Epistolary Fiction in Europe: 1500–1850* (Cambridge: Cambridge University Press, 1999), p. 50.
15 Jacques Lacan, *Écrits*, trans. Bruce Fink (New York: Norton, 2006), p. 18.
16 Jacques Lacan, *The Ethics of Psychoanalysis*, pp. 113–14.
17 John Locke, *A Paraphrase and Notes on the Epistles of St Paul to the Galations, 1 and 2 Corinthians, Romans, Ephesians*, ed. Arthur W. Wainwright, 2 vols. (Oxford: Oxford University Press, 1987), vol. I, p. 103.
18 Geoffrey Bennington, *Sententiousness and the Novel: Laying Down the Law in Eighteenth-Century French Fiction* (Cambridge: Cambridge University Press, 1985), pp. 17, 8, 56–7.
19 Quoted in T. C. Duncan Eaves and Ben D. Kimpel, *Samuel Richardson, a Biography* (Oxford: Clarendon, 1971), p. 420.
20 In early recognition of the sententiousness of Richardson's written style, Fielding adopts it for his *Shamela* (1741); see, for instance, Henry Fielding, *Joseph Andrews and Shamela*, ed. Douglas Brooks-Davies and Martin C. Battestin (Oxford: Oxford University Press, 1999), p. 319: 'O what a silly fellow is a bashful lover', although there are examples in virtually every letter.
21 On Lovelace's classical maxims, see Howard D. Weinbrot, *Menippean Satire Reconsidered: From Antiquity to the Eighteenth Century* (Baltimore, Md.: The Johns Hopkins University Press, 2005), pp. 286–7.
22 The outstanding version of the idea appears in Charlotte Lennox, *The Female Quixote; or The Adventures of Arabella*, printed by Richardson in 1752.
23 For a survey of this approach in twentieth-century criticism, see Terry Eagleton, *The Rape of Clarissa: Writing, Sexuality and Class Struggle in Samuel Richardson* (Oxford: Blackwell, 1982), pp. 63–70.
24 Even if the text does provide hints of that kind, it seems more important to affirm that Clarissa – like any of us – is entitled to have some contradiction and ambiguity in her desire without it implying any peculiar hypocrisy.

25 References to John Dryden and Nathaniel Lee, 'Oedipus: A Tragedy' in *The Works of John Dryden*, ed. H. T. Swedenberg Jr. and others, 20 vols. (Berkeley, Calif.: University of California Press, 1956–2002), vol. XIII, pp. 113–215.
26 Fielding, *Joseph Andrews and Shamela*, p. 295.
27 Castle, *Clarissa's Ciphers*, p. 85; Rachel Tricket, 'Dryden's Part in *Clarissa*', in Carol Houlihan Flynn and Edward Copeland (eds), *Clarissa and Her Readers: New Essays for the Clarissa Project* (New York: AMS, 1999), pp. 175–87 (p. 181).
28 Frances Sheridan, *Memoirs of Miss Sidney Bidulph*, ed. Patricia Köster and Jean Coates Cleary (Oxford: Oxford University Press, 1995), p. 50.
29 See Fielding, *Joseph Andrews and Shamela*, p. 35; for a related discussion of the humour of the scene, see William Empson, *Using Biography* (London: The Hogarth Press, 1984), p. 148.
30 George Etherege, *The Man of Mode; or, Sir Fopling Flutter*, in J. Douglas Canfield (ed.), *The Broadview Anthology of Restoration and Early Eighteenth Century Drama* (Ontario: Broadview, 2005), pp. 526–89.
31 John Gay, *The Beggar's Opera*, in J. Douglas Canfield (ed.), *The Broadview Anthology of Restoration and Early Eighteenth Century Drama* (Ontario: Broadview, 2005), pp. 1332–74.
32 See Lacan, *Écrits*, pp. 645–68.
33 Katherine Binhammer, *The Seduction Narrative in Britain, 1747–1800* (Cambridge: Cambridge University Press, 2009), p. 28.

2

During the afternoon and evening before he rapes Clarissa, Lovelace writes a letter to Belford that returns to the preoccupation with received notions we have seen runs through *Clarissa*'s early volumes:

> Is not *this* the hour of her trial – and in *her*, of the trial of the virtue of her whole sex, so long premeditated, so long threatened? – Whether her frost is frost indeed? Whether her virtue is principle? Whether, if *once subdued, she will not be always subdued*? And will she not want the very crown of her glory, the proof of her till now all-surpassing excellence, if I stop short of the ultimate trial? ... *Abhorred be force! – be the thoughts of force! There's no triumph over the will in force!* This I know I have said. But would I not have avoided it if I could? – Have I not tried every other method? And have I any other recourse left me? Can she resent the *last outrage* more than she has resented a *fainter effort*? – And if her resentments run ever so high, cannot I repair by matrimony? – She will not refuse me, Jack; the haughty beauty will not refuse me, when her pride of being corporally inviolate is brought down; when she can tell no tales, but when (be her resistance what it will) even her own sex will suspect a yielding in resistance; and when that modesty, which may fill her bosom with resentment, will lock up her speech. (C 879)

The habitual rakish maxim '*once subdued ... always subdued*' appears as Lovelace reassures himself that the rape will be retrospectively justified by Clarissa's subsequent sexual amenableness, and the familiar sentientious orthodoxy of the phrase is reinforced when it appears yet again in paraphrase later in the letter: 'as I have often said, *once forgiven, will be for ever forgiven*'. Failing this, Lovelace trusts that one of the other kinds of received notion we have examined – those formed in rumour – will bolster and smooth out his version of events, as what he had earlier called 'the *female round-about*' (C 85) sets in, and 'even her own sex will suspect a yielding in resistance'. Clarissa's pride in her virginity thus 'brought down', Lovelace assumes, she will bring all the fuss to a close by consenting to let him undo his wrongs 'by matrimony'.

Disturbingly neat as this plan seems, it is worth picking up on the fact that the assumption that Clarissa's actions can be anticipated with reference to maxims drawn from the evidence of the generality of women is actually the opposite of the other claim here that Clarissa's conduct after the rape will be 'the trial of the virtue of her whole sex': a measure by which to anticipate the behaviour of all women subsequently.[1] As well as this initial chiasmic fudging of argument, the letter is also marked by a quiet but significant unconscious repetition. In what will become nothing less than the dominating motif of this part of the novel, the prospect of the impending rape causes Lovelace to refer to both Clarissa and himself in some way interrupting themselves or breaking off mid-action: he in the idea that he might not go through with it – 'if I stop short of the ultimate trial' – and she – 'when she can tell no tales … lock[ing] up her speech' – in refusing or being unable to narrate it afterwards.

This little doubling up wouldn't stand out were it not for the famous note that Lovelace writes to Belford the following morning, after the rape has apparently taken place:

> AND now, Belford, I can go no farther. The affair is over. Clarissa lives. And I am
> Your humble servant,
> R. LOVELACE (C 883)

As Judith Wilt has argued, the phrase 'I can go no farther' acts as a kind of 'leitmotif governing much of Lovelace's thinking' at this stage of the novel. For Wilt, this abortive, interruptive phrase can be read alongside the emphasis the novel's subsequent fragmentary accounts of the rape place on the involvement in it of Mrs Sinclair and the other women, which together produce the provocative implication that Lovelace might be impotent and have left the rape uncompleted, at least without the assistance of the women. In so far as it has been taken seriously, the reading has been unsurprisingly controversial, but I'm less interested in weighing up Wilt's interpretation as an empirical statement about what 'really happens' in the novel than in taking the hint that there is something significant about the emergence of an emphasis on locking up speech, stopping short and going no further – the language, in short, of the caesura – in the novel's discourse at precisely this point.

It is after all worth remembering that Lovelace's two most successful actions in approaching Clarissa in the novel thus far have already been organised around versions of this gesture of interrupting or holding back. We have seen that Lovelace's initial courtship of Clarissa came of the trick of urbanely complying with the etiquette that requires elder sisters to be courted first, before playing the ingénue when it comes to that sister's equally conventional pretended refusal of him. Having put Bella out of temper by acting indifferently around her, Lovelace then imposes on her with an outright and swiftly 're-urged' (C 44) proposal such that she cannot possibly accept. 'And thus, as Mr Lovelace thought fit to *take it*', writes Clarissa, 'had he his answer from my sister'. Pretending to take the rejection as sincere, Lovelace is left free to decently turn his attentions to the younger sister. While some critics have regarded Lovelace as a proto-deconstructive deviant of linguistic play, he knows equally well the strategic power of good old literal-minded logocentrism.

A structurally similar trick is played by Lovelace in getting Clarissa to leave Harlowe Place. Facing the possibility that she is about to be forced into marrying Solmes in her own home, Clarissa writes to Lovelace one night towards the end of Volume II, finally capitulating to his suggestions that he should abduct her and take her to the protection of his family. Leaving the letter in the usual hiding place in the garden, Clarissa claims to have immediately regretted it, writing to Anna that she will 'take the letter back the first thing I do in the morning' (C 341). The letter, of course, has been taken by morning – 'what a strange diligence' (C 343) – and Clarissa writes again the following day limiting the terms under which she is willing to leave. This letter too – and again with 'strange diligence' (C 352) – is taken almost immediately: as Clarissa repeatedly puts it, 'the letter is out of my power' (C 343, 345, 352). Finally, regretting the whole thing, Clarissa writes again, 'a letter of revocation' (C 362), urging Lovelace not to come. But this letter Lovelace does not collect, and it lies in the same spot the entire day, Clarissa noting again and again how she has checked for it and found it uncollected. By this simple inaction in neglecting to take the third letter, Lovelace obligates Clarissa to meet him after all, and the abduction is effected. Once again, Lovelace is later able to play equivocally dumb: 'he was inexpressibly grieved and surprised, he said, to hear me say he had acted *artfully* by me', Clarissa writes, 'he came ... according to my *confirmed* appointment' (C 391).

But if interruption and inaction were on Lovelace's side earlier in the novel, things start to slip around the time of the rape. As Wilt remarks, from here on, 'most of the things [Lovelace] expects to happen do not happen'.[2] Lovelace may think he can anticipate Clarissa's behaviour on the basis of old received notions or use her conduct to form new ones, but the most important interruptions will now be those disrupting his own anticipations. We saw in Chapter 1 that, in the earlier parts of the novel, all kinds of authority have been neatly propped up by the self-validating magic of the various iterations of the received notion. But, as I argued in my introduction, the moment of the rape itself, caesural in its absence from the narrative, marks our entrance into a stranger landscape altogether, one much more in line with the fate of quotations and scholarly authorities in the damaged textual world Walter Benjamin identified with German baroque drama.

The remainder of this book is an examination of *Clarissa* in this tragic phase, but in this chapter I focus in particular on the major locus of this turn, the so-called 'mad papers', which appear shortly after Lovelace's enigmatic acknowledgement to Belford that the rape has taken place. Comprising a series of ten numbered passages, the mad papers veer from fragmentary allegorical narratives to half-formed letters with ambiguous addressees, to – in Paper X – scattered quotations, mainly from tragedies, which Clarissa writes down in her distracted state after the rape. This chapter begins by setting out a basis for understanding the mad papers with reference to some of the existing approaches that have been taken in discussing them. Following this, it makes specific case studies of three of Paper X's quotations from Thomas Otway, Shakespeare and Abraham Cowley to demonstrate the very different effect the logic of quotation is to be put to in this tragic phase of the novel.

I

The mad papers conclude with the remarkable Paper X, made up of bits of quotation printed by Richardson at haphazard angles on the page. The passages derive from Thomas Otway's tragedies *Venice Preserv'd* (1681) and *The Orphan* (1680), Shakespeare's *Hamlet* (c. 1600), Abraham Cowley's poem 'The Despair' from his collection of lyrics *The Mistress* (1656), Samuel Garth's satirical poem *The Dispensary* (1699) and Dryden's 'Palamon and Arcite', from *Fables Ancient and Modern* (1700), 'Absalom and Achitophel' (1681) and his plays, *The Indian Emperour* (1665), and *Oedipus* (1679), the last co-written with Nathaniel Lee, as we have seen.[3] Moving from Shakespeare to the metaphysicals, to Restoration drama and turn-of-the-century satire, the text is both a disorganised history of the seventeenth century and, in its preponderance on tragedies, a record of the period's representations of disaster: 'everything', as Benjamin would put it, 'untimely, sorrowful, unsuccessful'.[4] At the same time, it is, as *Clarissa*'s subtitle has it, an alternative 'history of a young lady', an autobiography and traumatic surrogate to the novel itself, even if its rapid changes of tense and implied address and the impossibility of insisting on any particular linear reading seem to frustrate any attempts to piece it together. How is Paper X to be read? In spite of the interest it has held for critics, Paper X has proven resistant to commentary and interpretation.

The mad papers are most often discussed as a reflection of the disordered state of Clarissa's mind, achieved both in the incoherence of the writing and, in Paper X specifically, the visual disorder of the printed page. 'The mutilation of sense and syntax', as one representative discussion puts it, 'is linked to a loss of selfhood'.[5] More recently, studies oriented towards the history of the book have focused on the challenge creating and publishing Paper X must have represented to Richardson as a printer and also on the way its material presentation on the page became a benchmark for visual experimentalism in the novels of the 1750s and after.[6] These arguments too have an emphasis on the mad papers as an achievement of verisimilitude: the high point of *Clarissa*'s capacity, says one critic, to 'periodically stray ... from its visual uniformity as a printed book in order to approximate graphically the look of original letters'.[7] Overall, these two approaches to the mad papers share an emphasis, first, on the extra-linguistic or formal aspect of Paper X (its fragmentariness or the technical innovativeness involved in producing it on the page) and, second, on verisimilitude (either of Clarissa's mindset or of the appearance of the fictional manuscript letters supposedly adapted into the printed novel). Revealingly though, in the thorough and ingenious world of Richardson scholarship, one is hard pressed to find much in the way of sustained critical reading of what Richardson actually has Clarissa write there.

The most detailed engagement with the 'content' of Paper X is an article by Michael E. Connaughton on the sources of its quotations. Because the article is generally referred to whenever the topic of Richardson's quotations comes up, and because the conclusions it draws are so peculiarly negative about Richardson, it is worth considering here. Building on observations first made by Alan D. McKillop and A. Dwight Culler in the 1930s and 1940s, Connaughton makes the fullest case for the extent to which Richardson seems to have drawn the quotations in Paper X and many of those in the novel generally from the sixth edition of Edward Bysshe's anthology *The Art of English Poetry* (1718) or one of its subsequent reprints.[8] First published in 1702, Bysshe's anthology appeared as a guide to the good writing of poetry, but its substantial collection of model poetic passages – arranged, like the *Collection* Richardson himself would eventually produce, alphabetically by theme – became by far the more influential part of the book throughout the eighteenth century.

Connaughton surmises Richardson's substantial reliance on Bysshe from the fact that *Clarissa* repeats fourteen misquotations also found in Bysshe, as well as some of his specific truncations of passages and, in one case, his erroneous attribution of a passage's authorship. Connaughton also shows that when Richardson's characters cite a passage they often do so in a context relevant to the thematic heading under which Bysshe had anthologised it. For Connaughton, all this is evidence of Richardson's slapdash 'unfamiliarity with the works quoted', and, worse, his 'amus[ing] ... vanity and pomposity', the effect of which is to substantially undermine the novel's achievement, at least as far as 'the art of allusion' is concerned. By way of illustration, Connaughton pursues several of the quotations in Paper X back to their sources, emphasising the apparently inappropriate satirical contexts of the passages from Garth and Dryden's 'Absalom and Achitophel', and the lack of immediate similarity between the situations from the Otway, Shakespeare and the Dryden and Lee plays. The problem of the relationship between the situation, the character and the choice of quotation, Connaughton suggests, 'indicates the insignificant role context plays in Richardson's thinking': 'a reader familiar with ... these passages in this situation could only ... view [them] as comic or [as] a serious breach of literary decorum'.[9]

There are, of course, some plausible mitigating circumstances to hand. Other critics who discuss Richardson's sources have assumed that he could easily have read the original texts and turned subsequently to Bysshe as a handy reminder when writing.[10] Authors such as Jonathan Swift and on occasion Richardson himself might have complained about 'this age of dictionary and index learning' where 'a smattering is almost all that is aimed at', but it is also worth stressing that our growing understanding of the role anthologies played in the eighteenth century's consumption of literature suggests that the application of quotations to not-obviously-relevant contexts may not have always been regarded as the 'breach of literary decorum' Connaughton feels it is.[11] But even without these qualifications, in what follows I want to take more seriously what is at stake in Clarissa's misquotations and indecorous identifications as the novel itself shows them being made. Serious breaches of literary decorum made by traumatised nineteen-year-olds days after a sexual assault are rather differently suggestive – and certainly less amusing – than those made by fashionable middle-aged novelists.

The dilemma is not very far from one voiced by Jacqueline Rose in *The Haunting of Sylvia Plath* (1991). Plath is perhaps the archetype of a poet whose work has been reduced to autobiography, with biographical explanations popularly standing in for criticism. For Rose, the work of redressing this means learning to read the poetry as if the identifications it makes and the subject positions it articulates are not always single, let alone always Plath herself: much as for William Empson, the speaker and addressee assumed within Ophelia's songs in *Hamlet* could frequently be more than one of the play's characters.[12] Rose contends that 'the idea of sequential development does not work' when it comes to reading Plath's poetry, which rather 'operates by means of repetitions, bits and pieces constantly reappearing, as if the poem were constructing the memory of itself' and 'as if Plath were offering a warning or responding in advance to those readers of her poetry who will battle it out over whom she really hated, or who is the real target of her rage'. Rose suggests that these multiple identifications need not be taken as announcements of consciously held or committed to emotional position but are better understood as belonging to a poetry that 'addresses the production of fantasy as such'.[13] 'The production of fantasy as such' is a helpful phrase for avoiding the temptation to either sidestep Paper X's obscurity altogether by finding significance only in its formal presentation or, indeed, to complain of lack of correspondence between the specific circumstances of Clarissa as its author and the speakers of these statements in their source texts. It will also enable us to see quite how far at this point in the novel's tragic phase the function of quotation has changed from what it was in the novel's first volumes.

II

The rough column of verse at the heart of Paper X starts by quoting Otway's *Venice Preserv'd*, returning to the play in the fourth of its haphazard stanzas, where a second passage is truncated with one from *The Orphan*, another of Otway's tragedies. Clarissa is supposed to have discussed *Venice Preserv'd* in a 'little book' written at Anna's behest 'upon the principal acting plays' (C 640) – among those alluring Borges-like texts Richardson's reader is referred to but never gets to see – and we know that Clarissa has also seen the play performed with Lovelace a few weeks earlier. On that occasion, Lovelace suggests a comparison between Clarissa and the play's heroine, Belvidera, much as Belford will later make one between Clarissa and another heroine of the so-called 'she-tragedies' of the turn of the century: Calista from Nicholas Rowe's *The Fair Penitent* (1702) (C 1205–6). Watching Otway's play is supposed 'to show her', Lovelace says, 'that there have been, and may be, much deeper distresses than she can possibly know' (C 620). In Otway's play, these 'deeper distresses' begin when Belvidera is cut off by her father, Priuli, after her clandestine marriage to Jaffeir, a penurious nobleman who subsequently falls in with a group of plotters against the Venetian Senate. Belvidera ends up being left with the plotters as an assurance that Jaffeir will not renege on their plan, during which time she narrowly avoids being raped. After much intrigue and the dishonourable failure of the conspiracy, Jaffeir takes his own life, leaving Belvidera to enter the stage to 'soft music', speaking in mad fractured terms of mourning, accusation and bawdiness by turn.[14]

Belvidera disobeys her father, comes close to rape and ends up resembling the Restoration and eighteenth century's preferred icon of female madness, *Hamlet*'s Ophelia, so it would not be surprising to find Clarissa resorting to the precedent in her own, superficially similar, crisis.[15] In turn, this would suggest the parallel between the triad of Clarissa–Lovelace–James Harlow Senior and that of Belvidera–Jaffeir–Priuli. As neat as this seems, the problem is that when *Venice Preserv'd* appears in Paper X, Clarissa is actually quoting not from Belvidera but from Jaffeir. Connaughton may speak for whatever readers of Richardson have recognised the provenance of the passages – in the days of the play's broad popularity it was not impossible – when he counts them among Richardson's embarrassing faux pas caused by his careless reliance on Bysshe.[16] But perhaps things are not as simple as they seem. What if the problem raised by Paper X at this point is the more fundamental one of what counts as a 'proper' identification? When the expectation would clearly be that Clarissa should quote Belvidera (and Lovelace has already suggested the similarity of the two), what is articulated in the slip that leads to her quoting Jaffeir? Taking the question in this way may help us see that the procedure of Paper X is not to engage in the classical use of citation as a sort of shorthand – a production of mottos proper to their subjects – but rather, like Plath's poetry in Rose's analysis, to open out 'the production of fantasy as such'. Paper X is a document in the acceptance of fantasy's demand that counter-intuitive identifications be made, that rival subject positions be simultaneously explored and even persecutors tentatively identified with, whatever the risk to either literary decorum or the self-consistency of the subject herself.

The acceptance of this enigmatic dimension of fantasy that we can find implied in Paper X marks the first major shift in the function of quotation in the novel. The text has gone from using quotation as a means of recycling and reinforcing identity-fixing received notions, as examined in Chapter 1, to a conception that occupies Benjamin's and Lacan's respective grounds for talking about tragedy simultaneously. The citation is starting to become allegorical, an enigmatic constellation, like the mosaics referred to at the start of Benjamin's *Trauerspiel* book: its repetitions are now to be understood as productive of difference, not sameness.[17] At the same time, the apparent lack of subjective consistency in Paper X may recall Lacan's sense of the ethical in *Antigone*, the heroine's commitment to the anti-subjective vicissitudes of the drive at the cost of anything recognisably human. This, as much as its sudden schizoid cuts and citations from actual tragic dramas, marks Paper X as a document of the caesura and of the tragic.

Paper X begins:

> LEAD me, where my own thoughts themselves may lose me;
> Where I may doze out what I've left of life,
> Forget myself; and that day's guilt! –
> Cruel remembrance! – how shall I appease thee? (C 893)[18]

In *Venice Preserv'd*, this is Jaffeir's statement of remorse after he has betrayed his friends and fellow plotters against Venice at Belvidera's behest. Clarissa begins speaking not from the point of view of the trauma of the woman, but of the man. If on some level she recognises the triadic association between Jaffeir and Lovelace, it is as if she consents to begin by speaking as if she were Lovelace, attributing to him in fantasy Jaffeir's horror at his own act of betrayal. At the same time, if she retains the more obvious association between herself and Belvidera, then she is no longer the woman betrayed but the woman who has had some agency in a betrayal committed by a man against other men. Whatever Richardson's intentions (or lack of them), the effect of this quotation is to allow all this compressed work of fantasy into the text. Clarissa both identifies with and obscurely attributes remorse to her tormentor, while wrestling some however flawed trace of agency for herself.

There is another important way in which Richardson's choice of an apparently inappropriate quotation opens out something more searching and unstable than the kinds of received notion-fixing quotation that dominated the earlier parts of the novel. Returning to Otway's play after reading Paper X puts one in a position to notice that the solicitation 'lead me' is actually made oddly frequently in it. While the lines Paper X quotes derive from Jaffeir's lament at his eventual betrayal of the plotters, his commitment to them in the first place has already been figured as an instance of 'leading' when his friend Pierre first tempts him to join the 'council … where the destruction / of this great empire's hatching', promising 'there I'll lead thee!'.[19] After Belvidera convinces Jaffeir to betray the plotters, Jaffeir seems to remember Pierre's phrase while melancholically imagining his friend's body torn to pieces: 'where dost thou lead me? Every step I move / methinks I tread upon some mangled limb / of a racked friend'.[20] As much as Clarissa's 'lead me' may carry in fantasy form a number of compressed conflicting attitudes towards Lovelace, for Jaffeir, 'lead me' is the clue phrase for his joining the plot, his betraying it and finally his despondency after betraying it simultaneously: all are identified as analogous instances of 'leading'. Yet further, Belvidera's own first lines (to her attendants) are 'lead me, lead me my virgins / to that kind voice!', and in the same conversation she asks Jaffeir to 'lead me to some desert wide and wild'.[21] The phrase is also Priuli's, who, in *Trauerspiel* mode and anticipating Clarissa's word 'mourn' in Paper X's third stanza, says towards the play's end, 'lead me into some place that's fit for mourning'.[22] In a play written in the fraught context of the 1670s and 1680s, wracked by political conspiracy theories, it seems there is no affect that cannot be figured as a kind of seduction, a dangerous 'leading astray'. Paper X meanwhile may cite Jaffeir's lines, but it cannot be said to limit itself to the single identification with Jaffeir at this specific moment in the play. Rather, it allows for identifications with the various conflicting meanings it has for Jaffeir, with the several other characters who also use the phrase at key moments and, finally, simply the structural position of *the subject who is led* itself: the importance of which in *Venice Preserv'd* Clarissa must now be assumed to have registered in her previous dealings with the play.

A further twist can be found in the intimations the phrase may have picked up between Otway's time and Richardson's. Abstracted out of the continuous dialogue of the source play and repositioned at the head of what looks like a column of verse, this opening for Paper X also has overtones quite specific to the 1740s. The poetry of that decade repeatedly evokes Milton's Christian recasting of the Homeric invocation to the muses in *Paradise Lost*'s 'Sing Heav'nly Muse' and the similar invocations in the 'Christ's Nativity' ode and *Lycidas*. While Milton only comes close to formulating this specifically in terms of 'leading' in Samson's ambiguously directed opening line in *Samson Agonistes* – 'a little onward lend thy guiding hand / to these dark steps, a little further on' – the Miltonic poetry of the 1740s produces more explicit examples.[23] Joseph Warton's 'The Enthusiast; or, The Lover of Nature' (1740) begins by soliciting the 'green-rob'd dryads' to 'lead me from the gardens deck'd with art's vain pomps'.[24] Edward Young's *Night Thoughts*, printed by Richardson in 1742, addresses sleep as an inspiration for poetry in a similar way: 'O lead my mind ... Lead it thro' various scenes of *Life* and *Death*'.[25] And, in 1746, the speaker of William Collins's 'Ode to Evening' makes yet another similar invocation: 'lead, calm vot'ress, where some sheety lake / Cheers the lone heath'.[26] If we take the hint from its visual presentation that Paper X might be treated as a peculiar kind of poetry, the opening statement 'lead me' becomes transformed into a conventional way of introducing a poem. Clarissa is not simply scrawling these quotations at random: she is scrambling to write a poem consistent with the 1740s Miltonic mode.

In these several ways, we can only comfortably dismiss Richardson's apparently arbitrary choice of quotation from Otway by overlooking the surreptitiously searching work it does in breaking open new meanings in the source text and the enigmatic alternative identifications it presents at the level of Clarissa's work of fantasy. That said, if the most straightforward available interpretation of why Clarissa should cite these lines at this point would be something along the lines of her aspiring to a place or situation where the rape's pernicious mental effects may be alleviated by forgetfulness, then there is a final issue that needs to be accounted for. While we have seen how significant the motif of 'leading' evidently is in *Venice Preserv'd*, where is it in *Clarissa*? Writing at the start of the second instalment, shortly after her abduction by Lovelace, Clarissa exclaims:

> Oh the vile encroacher! how my indignation, at times rises at him! Thus to lead a young creature (too much indeed relying upon her own strength) from evil to evil! – This last evil, although the remote, yet sure consequence of my first – my prohibited correspondence! by a father, at least, early prohibited! (C 381)

Surely the novel's own most significant example of 'leading' is this: Clarissa's earlier insistence that the transgression of writing against her parents' consent has led directly to the more grievous one of consenting to be led away from Harlowe Place by Lovelace? The dramatic weight of this instance of leading and leaving at the turn of the second instalment is emphasised, we may add, by the fact that Richardson introduces the third instalment with an analogous incident. Towards the end of the fourth volume, Clarissa escapes from Lovelace's captivity at Mrs Sinclair's house to Hampstead, and Lovelace decries her departure – 'Zounds, man, the lady is gone off!' (C 736) – in language directly recalling Clarissa's announcement of having 'gone off with a man' (C 370), which marked her departure *with* Lovelace at the end of Volume II. In the event, one does not have to read terribly far in the following volume to find Lovelace successfully retrieving her. But nonetheless, that both the second and the third and final instalment of the novel begin in the flux of Clarissa having just escaped somewhere underlines the structural importance that Clarissa's first talk of 'leading' in the passage from the third volume quoted above has for the rhythm of the novel. That letter goes on to ask, 'can I give a sanction immediately to his deluding arts? – can I *avoid* being angry with him for tricking me thus, as I may say (and as I have called it to him), out of myself? – for compelling me to take a step so contrary to all my resolutions' (C 382).

Clarissa's 'resolutions' here are presumably those referred to in her account of the events immediately prior to her meeting Lovelace and leaving Harlowe Place: 'I congratulated myself, that I had resolved against going away with Mr Lovelace' (C 373). This, finally, is the scandalously counter-intuitive act of fantasy permitted by Paper X. Our initial common-sense reading of its opening quotation as representing Clarissa wishing to be led out of herself into some forgetfulness of the traumatic event cannot stand because that wish is being presented in language that at every turn calls back the very circumstances of leaving with Lovelace that precipitated the traumatic event in the first place.

III

The second citation in Paper X comes from Hamlet's accusation to Gertrude in her closet over her marriage to Claudius. Spoken in the confusion following Hamlet's ambiguously accidental killing of Polonius, Hamlet charges his mother with committing

> such an act
> That blurs the grace and blush of modesty,
> Calls virtue hypocrite, takes off the rose
> From the fair forehead of an innocent love
> And sets a blister there
>
> (III.iv.39–43)

The point seems transparent enough in the running of the scene, but the slower attention demanded by our wondering why the passage is supposed to have stood out to Clarissa reveals that the lines are already rather confusing, even before the problems they accrue in being cited in Paper X are taken into account. If we insist on taking Shakespeare's figurative language at its word, we realise Hamlet's accusation does not make it clear whether the 'act' Gertrude has performed has actively spoiled a state of innocence or simply revealed it to have never been that innocent at all.

First, modesty's 'grace and blush', we are told, have been 'blurred' by the act. 'Grace and blush' is a hendiadys – one of *Hamlet*'s habitual rhetorical devices – breaking the adjective and noun in the expected phrase, 'graceful blush', into two separate nouns.[27] Common as this is in *Hamlet*, the effect here is to inadvertently activate a double meaning in 'blurred'. The *Oxford English Dictionary* quotes the passage as its first citation for 'blur' in the sense of 'disfigure, befoul, defile', but, equally, we may hear the other meaning (also a Shakespearean first citation): 'to make indistinct', to blur together, 'as writing is by being blurred'. So either Gertrude has 'blurred the grace and blush of modesty' in the probably intended sense of ruining its once 'graceful blush', or, since the hendiadys has made grace and blush into two separate properties, the problem is that while they were fine in themselves, they have been ruined by being improperly blurred together. Either goodness has been spoiled from outside or its despoliation was already implicit in the properties it had to begin with.

This might seem needlessly finicky, but which reading wins out has material implications for Clarissa's reaching for the passage at this point in the novel. When Hamlet says that Gertrude's act has 'called virtue hypocrite', he is being similarly ambiguous. Calling someone a hypocrite is not the same as demonstrating them to be so, so the question becomes whether the accusation of hypocrisy the 'act' is supposed to have directed at virtue is warranted or not. Either Gertrude's unvirtuous act has falsely cast aspersion on virtue in general, or, more grievously, it has exposed virtue for never having been what it said it was in the first place. The passage's final image of setting a blister on 'the fair forehead of an innocent love' has precisely the same problem. While this might seem like a reasonably unambiguous act of despoliation, actually it is made more puzzling by the fact that, as most editors point out, the image is drawn from the apocryphal Elizabethan practice of branding prostitutes on the forehead: a physical staining marking an already existing moral one.[28] At every turn in the passage, Hamlet's charge that Gertrude has ruined something won't quite give up on the transgressive possibility that it was already ruined to begin with.

As with the *Venice Preserv'd* citation, it is also not immediately clear why Clarissa should be quoting these lines. Like Belvidera, Ophelia is Clarissa's more obvious analogue, yet she quotes Hamlet speaking of and to the other main female character in the play. At a time when the 'real' loss of Clarissa's virginity is at stake – as Lovelace unpleasantly puts it 'when her pride of being corporally inviolable is brought down' (C 879) – she quotes lines that sound like they are about virginity but actually are so only figuratively: Hamlet is pointedly saying that the corrupting loss of virginity is only *like* Gertrude's premature remarriage. This stubborn seizing on *Hamlet*'s manifest figurative language rather than on what it strictly 'means' becomes perfectly legible, however, if we read it as a response taking place at the level of fantasy. For does not the ambivalence we have identified in Hamlet's original lines over whether something has been ruined or merely exposed as being corrupted already precisely repeat Lovelace's terms for thinking of the rape of Clarissa as a kind of test or trial? It was Lovelace who raised the question 'whether her frost is frost indeed? Whether her virtue is principle?' (C 879), and, with this in mind, we can say that Clarissa's choice of quotation in fact comes perilously close to interiorising the terms set by Lovelace over this 'trial'. This would suggest rather grimly that Clarissa submits to Lovelace's terms for framing the question even as she raids *Hamlet* for lines with which to accuse him. In *Hamlet*, 'frost' is not necessarily 'frost': 'virtue' can be a pose rather than 'principle'.

Yet in keeping with the dynamics of this fractured fantasy writing, we can also take the quotation in another way. What if the implication of the split in Hamlet's lines is not merely that of an inadvertent self-blame on Clarissa's part analogous to the guilt often felt by rape survivors today but rather a deconstructive refusal to settle on the conventional opposition between pure and impure, chaste and unchaste, virgin and non-virgin in which Lovelace is trying to set the question? This would mean contending, as Shakespeare puts it elsewhere, that 'there is not enough chastity in language' (*Much Ado About Nothing*, IV.i.96) for us to find any secure way of maintaining such divisions in discourse. The secret articulation of the *Hamlet* lines is that there is no position of prior purity: it can only be spoken of retrospectively from a position that is always already assumed to be corrupted.[29] So Clarissa's quotation of Shakespeare in Paper X raises the possibility of identifying with Lovelace's view of the rape, only to surreptitiously offer a conceptual vocabulary for resisting it.

Significantly, this pattern applies to much of the Shakespeare quotation in *Clarissa* in general. Later in the novel, when Clarissa has finally escaped from Lovelace, he recalls to Belford that she is 'well read in Shakespeare, our English pride and glory', adding that she 'must sometimes reason with herself in his words' (C 1148). Lovelace then quotes Claudio's 'Ay, but to die and go we know not where' speech from *Measure for Measure* (III.i.118–32), applying it to the question of whether Clarissa's 'innate piety' will 'permit her to shorten her own life, either by violence or neglect' (C 1148). The letter is sometimes quoted approvingly in discussions of Richardson's engagement with Shakespeare, but what is less often emphasised is that this is not so much Clarissa reasoning with herself in Shakespeare's words as Lovelace assuming to do that reasoning for her. Notwithstanding the suspicion with which all of Lovelace's attempts to psychologise Clarissa ought to be taken, Lovelace himself actually draws attention to a limitation in this conventional idea that literary quotations are somehow a useful way for us to express things about ourselves that we would struggle to put 'in our own words'. After quoting *Measure for Measure*, Lovelace acknowledges that Shakespeare's language is 'so greatly expressed' that the situation it is being applied to, 'affecting as it is, cannot produce anything more so'. The meandering confusion of real life cannot compete with the monumentalising language of Shakespeare, citation from which overburdens what we seek to clarify. Much as Lovelace had hoped Clarissa's identification with the events of *Venice Preserv'd* would make her overlook her own troubles in light of the severity of Belvidera's, reasoning in Shakespeare quotations may seem to aid or supplement the dilemma the person wants to communicate or reconcile, but it also risks letting the citation replace the situation being thought through altogether.

Lacan makes a similar point in discussing the tendency of his analysands to make 'reference to a passage from the Bible, to an author, whether classic or not, or to some piece of music' at the very moment in an analysis when they are approaching the most crucial part of the issue at hand.[30] Despite Lacan's own notoriously mandarin scope of allusion, his point is that such references do not help his analysands to say what they need to say but rather offer a way of avoiding doing so. The references tend to come up 'at the very moment that a thought is clearly about to appear in a subject ... that one recognises as aggressive relative to one of the fundamental terms of his subjective constellation', allowing instead the 'subjective constellation' – identity as usual – to carry on undisrupted. At the moment self-examination drifts too close to something unacceptable to oneself, that is the moment to seize upon some reassuringly clever analogy for one's experience, and so the encounter is missed. This is not as simple as saying that the analysand's meaning is completely lost as a result of this diversion, however. 'You can be sure', Lacan stresses, 'that the more these references become strangely sporadic and peremptory ... the more they are correlative of something that makes its presence felt at that moment, and that belongs to the register of a destructive drive'. The mere fact that these anomalous imported passages have appeared in the analysand's discourse at all is a signal that things have come too close to the bone, that something of the order of the death drive is under way, and this is obliquely significant in itself. According to Benjamin, 'the corpse' became in the seventeenth century 'the preeminent emblematic property', as if the breakage between sign and sense in the period's allegorical artworks always had something deathly about it, whatever other official purpose the form might be being put to.[31] Similarly, we can say, the different possibilities of what exactly Clarissa is supposed to be reasoning in Shakespeare's words when she quotes him are all very well (this chapter has clearly set plenty of store by them), but all of these fractured and interrupting quotations have the ultimate referent of a certain deathliness inscribed in their mere presence.

The complex situation of the *Hamlet* quotation is not made simpler by the alterations the passage undertakes in the process of transcription. In *Clarissa* the passage appears as this:

> – Oh! you have done an act
> That blots the face and blush of modesty;
>   Takes off the rose
> From the fair forehead of an innocent love,
> And makes a blister there! –

Clarissa's replacement of Shakespeare's 'blurs the grace' with 'blots the face' is a misquotation found in Bysshe, but the excision of 'calls virtue a hypocrite' is Richardson's own.[32] The latter alteration may suggest a repression in Clarissa: the previous Paper VIII has affirmed her honesty – 'God knows my heart, I had no culpable inclinations! – I honoured virtue!' (C 892) – and whatever the extent of her self-accusation here and in other parts of the novel, and whatever the frenzy of this act of mad writing, she seems to back away from including the possibility that she has been hypocritical in her dealings with Lovelace. The first alteration is more suggestive. From the blush to the blur to the blister, Shakespeare's version gave three images of progressively exacerbated marking, a metonymic series of kinds of blemish or stain. While we have seen that Shakespeare's 'blur' has an intimation of writing in it in the word's relationship to smeared ink, Clarissa's innovation in replacing blur with 'blot' in her misremembered transcription is to make the writerly aspect of the metaphor even more explicit, adding another stain to the series the passage already presented.

It is worth concluding this consideration of the passage by recalling that the association between moral staining and ink has been made at an important juncture in the novel already. Like so much in the mad papers, Clarissa is not simply reasoning with herself in Shakespeare's words or drawing an appropriate analogy between her situation and one from classic literature, but instead may be said to be re-performing the terms of some element of her suffering in an unexpected fantasised form. Early in the novel's dealing with the Harlowes' persecution of Clarissa, their servant, Betty, uses a trick to discover that Clarissa has, against her family's orders, been writing letters. Clarissa writes that 'the saucy creature took a napkin, and dipped it in water, and with a fleering air: Here miss: holding the wet corner to me' (C 344–5). Taking the corner, Clarissa inadvertently stains the napkin with the hitherto disguised ink on her fingers. Just as for Lacan a seemingly irrelevant quotation or comparison used in place of an actual admission in analysis has a significance simply in being there, the ink stain – though unreadable in itself – gives the proof that writing has been taking place. We saw in the previous chapter that much of the oppression of Clarissa by her family at that stage of the novel is propped up by the apparent stability given to their received notions by their repetition. Here, as it were, in Clarissa's recasting that inkblot into Hamlet's list of stains is an instance of the new kind of quotation represented in the mad papers looking back and casting judgement on the old. Certainly, the subdued absurdity of calling someone 'saucy', for insolent, in the context of describing a stained napkin hardly suggests that language is something rigidly under control.

IV

It should be clear by now that Richardson's indecorous choices of quotations cannot simply be dismissed as irrelevant to the plot or to Clarissa's situation, and, further, that at this point in the novel the entire function of quotation has changed. Something has happened around the caesural moment of the rape which means that quotation can thereafter never be relied upon to simply perpetuate received notions as it did before. As a final demonstration, I consider here Paper X's third passage (space and readerly patience constrain me from discussing them all), derived from the third and fourth verses of Abraham Cowley's poem, 'The Despair'.

'The Despair' appeared in *The Mistress*, Cowley's collection of love lyrics of 1647. The section Clarissa makes use of is in bold:

> Beneath this gloomy shade,
> By nature only for my sorrows made,
> I'll spend this voice in cries,
> In tears I'll waste these *eyes*
> By *love* so vainly fed;
> So *lust* of old the deluge punished.
> *Ah wretched youth*, said I!
> *Ah wretched youth*! twice did I sadly cry:
> *Ah wretched youth*! the fields and floods reply.
> When thoughts of love I entertain,
> I meet no words but *never*, and *in vain*.
> Never (alas) that dreadful name,
> Which fuels the infernal flame:
> *Never*, my time to come must waste;
> *In vain*, torments the present, and the past.
> *In vain, in vain*! said I;
> *In vain*! In *vain*! twice did I sadly cry;
> *In vain*! In *vain*! the fields and floods reply.
> No more shall fields or floods do so;
> For I to shades more dark and silent go:
> All this world's noise appears to me
> A dull ill-acted *comedy*:
> No comfort to my wounded sight,
> In the sun's busy and impertinent light.
> **Then down I laid my head,**
> **Down on cold earth; and for a while was dead,**
> **And my freed *soul* to a strange *somewhere* fled.**
> Ah sottish *soul*; said I,
> When back t'his cage again I saw it fly:
> **Fool to resume his *broken chain*!**
> **And row his *galley* here again!**
> **Fool, to that body to return**
> **Where it condemn'd and destin'd is to *burn*!**
> Once *dead*, how can it be,
> *Death* should a thing so pleasant seem to thee,
> That thou shouldst come to *live it o'er again* in *me*?[33]

Cowley makes the same separation of body and soul as Andrew Marvell's slightly later 'A Dialogue between the Soul and the Body', but whereas Marvell has the body speak belligerently against the 'tyrannic soul' and the soul resent being 'shipwrecked' in the body, Cowley's speaker rebukes the soul for wishing to stay with the body and does not allow the body a separate persona.[34] The section quoted by Clarissa welcomes a momentary death, possibly in sleep (linking with the *Venice Preserv'd* lines about wanting to 'doze out what I've left of life') followed by a return to life in waking. But after the prevaricating adjoining passage in which the soul is 'freed ... to a strange *somewhere*' before returning, the soul is charged with being 'sottish', stupid, for coming back to the body and dooming both yet again to miserable life. Cowley's version then concludes with a last twist of metaphysical wit. The soul is charged with having perversely found '*Death* ... a thing so pleasant' that it wished to '*live it o'er again*': to die once more at the eventual 'real' death of the speaker, who, yet more grimly, is thereafter 'destin'd ... to *burn*'.

Richardson seems to have regarded Cowley as a minority interest in the 1740s, 'out of fashion in this age of taste' and as such 'absolutely neglected'.[35] He would have found this passage in Bysshe under the heading 'Death', and, in turn, Samuel Johnson may have been influenced by Richardson's inclusion of it in Paper X, when in his study of Cowley he cited precisely the same extract under the title 'A Lover Neither Dead nor Alive', in illustration of how the 'thoughts and expressions' of the metaphysical poets 'were sometimes grossly absurd, and such as no figures or license can reconcile to the understanding'.[36] As is generally the case in his readings of poetry, Johnson is perfectly right, if not necessarily for the right reasons. The poem is absurd, exaggerated and ostentatious and certainly does not 'reconcile to understanding' if by that we mean that it is impossible to reduce it to a single paraphrased idea. When Richardson copied the extract from Bysshe, the gender of the soul had already been conveniently if rather mysteriously changed: 'fool! to resume her broken Chain'.[37] The last line quoted in Paper X appearing as 'destin'd is to *burn*' in both

Cowley and in Bysshe, however, suggests that the change to 'destin'd is to *mourn*' is Richardson's own. Perhaps replacing 'burn' with 'mourn' – like the excision of 'calls virtue hypocrite' in the *Hamlet* passage – can be thought of as a small act of repression on Clarissa's part, as if she doesn't wish to go so far as to allow the possibility of the rape sealing her for damnation. But if this is so, the fact that, alone in the passage, the word '*mourn*' is italicised and indeed spoils the rhyme draws attention to the very thing that Paper X was apparently working to disguise. If the line's starting with the condemnation of the soul means that Cowley's 'burn' might well be anticipated as the rhyme for 'return' anyway, then Richardson actually has it both ways, saying '*mourn*' but allowing 'burn' to echo itself through as well.

As was the case with Clarissa's use of the 'lead me' lines from *Venice Preserv'd*, the selection and this small change means that we return to the source text with a slightly altered sense of what it has to say. Once again, Paper X refuses to treat its source texts as stable authorities ready to be borrowed from at a convenient moment and instead effects a violent clash of discourses from which neither emerges unchanged. If Clarissa makes the speaker to whom the soul returns destined to mourn rather than to burn, then we may come to see how the poem foregrounds an unusual kind of mourning already. From the start, the speaker has established himself as one 'by nature only for my sorrows made', suggesting that sorrow is natural – an originary state – and that there was never a time when one was not in mourning. But as much as he was formed by it and for it, mourning also threatens to break the speaker apart, as he imagines his voice and eyes dissolving themselves in crying and tears: 'I'll spend this voice in cries / In tears I'll waste these *eyes*'. Spending the voice suggests destroying it, but it also seems to multiply it, as the speaker repeats his lament '*Ah wretched youth*', only to have it repeated back to him by nature itself, represented by 'the floods and fields'. This mourning that makes and unmakes the subject, precedes him in nature and – in Paper X's version – is all s/he can anticipate of the future, is wholly consistent with

Benjamin's interpretation of the significance of mourning in the seventeenth century. For Benjamin

> nature remained the great teacher for the writers of this period. However, nature was not seen by them in bud and bloom, but in the over-ripeness and decay of her creations. In nature they saw eternal transience, and here alone did the saturnine vision of this generation recognise history. Its monuments, ruins, are ... the home of the saturnine beasts.[38]

In Benjamin's seventeenth century, the conventional oppositions of nature and history, plenitude and decay, do not apply. We do not mourn something that has been materially lost, but rather mourning precedes and casts its shadow on all human achievement. There is no 'bud and bloom' for nature prior to the ruinous touch of history, just as there was no time of plenitudinous wholeness to be subsequently mourned. Culture's monuments were always ruins, and the beasts themselves were always in mourning. Influenced by Benjamin's interpretation of the period in his *Doktor Faustus*, Thomas Mann finds this universal mourning in Monteverdi's opera, *L'Arianna* (1608): 'Monteverdi ... favoured the echo-effect, sometimes to the point of being a mannerism. The echo, the giving back of the human voice as nature-sound, and the revelation of it *as* nature-sound is essentially a lament'. Just as in Cowley's echoing 'floods and fields', for Mann, the 'echo, favourite device of the baroque, is employed with unspeakably mournful effect'.[39]

Clarissa's placing mourning in the subject's future destiny as well as her past exaggerates what for Benjamin and Mann would be a messing with the temporality of mourning already present in the baroque Cowley's original. But time is at stake in the poem in another way, which, again, Paper X's exploratory use of the quotation serves to bring out. In Paper X, the lines represent a noticeably jarring change of tense, moving from the present tense address of the *Hamlet* passage to the past tense of Cowley: 'Then down I laid my head'. This might be expected in a piece of writing dragged together from various plays and poems, but, returning to the source poem, we realise that the tense is all over the place in Cowley already. It jumps from speaking non-specifically of the future – 'I'll spend this voice in cries' – and the present – 'When thoughts of love I entertain' – to speaking as if all this happened in the past: 'Then down I laid my head'. The poem's comment on its ongoing despair, '*Never*, my time to come must waste / *In vain*, torments the present, and the past', is replicated at the level of these disorientating changes of tense which makes the time of the 'Then' marking the soul's escape impossible to date. If the logic of Cowley's poem already says that mourning has thrown out of kilter any sense of time, then Paper X's small change of 'destin'd is to *mourn*' simply extends this logic, projecting mourning into the furthest future.

Such difficulties of reconciling the poem to any final understanding are, in Johnson's negative appraisal, part of its metaphysical trait, and Paper X's accumulation of internally and mutually contradictory citations more widely only works further to drive this to its natural conclusion. Indeed, Paper X's dislocated citations can be seen as a peculiarly literal case of Johnson's famous dictum that in metaphysical poetry 'the most heterogeneous ideas are yoked by violence together'.[40] But the qualities Johnson disparages as metaphysical are those Benjamin claims for the baroque, referring to 'the relationship between mourning and ostentation, which is so brilliantly displayed in the language of the baroque'.[41] This, finally, is what we can call the baroque mode of the mad papers. They cannot be expected to produce a single psychological statement which could be reconciled 'to the understanding', because their mode is an ostentatious overloading of significance and reference, both in the aggressive readings their juxtapositions and misquotations make of their source texts and the multiple significances they seem to have for the dilemmas of the novel itself. The final articulation of these citations, as their parallels with Benjamin and Lacan in their very different ways suggest, is the tragic one of the recognition of something deathly or mournful. The instrumental function given to citation in the earlier part of the novel has been overthrown in this caesural space of the rape and the confused mournfulness of these passages is what begins to bear this out.

Notes

1 Lovelace has been proposing this idea since early in the novel's second instalment (C 427).
2 Wilt, 'He Could Go No Farther'; quotations taken from the subsequent exchange between Robert M. Schulz and Judith Wilt, 'Lovelace and Impotence', *PMLA*, 92 (5) (1977): 1005–6 (pp. 1005, 1006).
3 Most of these references are identified by Angus Ross (C 1520nL261), with additional identifications made in Samuel Richardson, *Clarissa: an Abridged Edition*, ed. Toni Bowers and John Richetti (Ontario: Broadview, 2011), p. 483n1.
4 Benjamin, *The Origin of German Tragic Drama*, p. 166.
5 Castle, *Clarissa's Ciphers*, p. 120; compare John Preston, *The Created Self: The Reader's Role in Eighteenth-Century Fiction* (London: Heinemann, 1970), p. 49: 'Clarissa's state of mind is represented as the disintegration of a book'; and Keymer, *Richardson's Clarissa and the Eighteenth-Century Reader*: 'the fragmentation, both syntactic and material, attests a crisis in which language can no longer encompass life' (p. 224).
6 See Stephanie Fysh, *The Work(s) of Samuel Richardson* (Newark, Del.: University of Delaware Press, 1997), Chapter 4; Steven R. Price, 'The Autograph Manuscript in Print: Samuel Richardson's Type Font Manipulation in Clarissa', in Paul C. Gutjahr and Megan L Benton (eds), *Illuminating Letters: Typography and Literary Interpretation* (Amherst, Mass.: University of Massachusetts Press, 2001), pp. 115–35; Janine Barchas, *Graphic Design, Print Culture, and the Eighteenth-Century Novel* (Cambridge: Cambridge University Press, 2003), p. 16; Thomas Keymer, *Sterne, the Moderns and the Novel* (Oxford: Oxford University Press, 2002), p. 67; these are anticipated in an earlier discussion by Geoffrey Day, *From Fiction to the Novel* (London and New York: Routledge, 1987), pp. 92–3.
7 Barchas, *Graphic Design*, p. 131.
8 Alan D. McKillop, *Samuel Richardson, Printer and Novelist* (Chapel Hill, NC: University of North Carolina Press, 1936),

p. 141; A. Dwight Culler 'Edward Bysshe and the Poet's Handbook', *PMLA*, 63 (3) (1948), 858–85 (p. 871); see also Eaves and Kimpel, *Samuel Richardson*, p. 572.

9 Michael E. Connaughton, 'Richardson's Familiar Quotations: *Clarissa* and Bysshe's Art of English Poetry', *Philological Quarterly*, 60 (2) (1981), 183–95 (pp. 183, 184, 186, 188).

10 Most prominently Jocelyn Harris, 'Richardson: Original or Learned Genius?' in Margaret Anne Doody and Peter Sabor (eds), *Samuel Richardson: Tercentenary Essays*, ed. (Cambridge: Cambridge University Press, 1989), pp. 188–202; for other positive examinations of Richardson's use of his sources, see Valerie Grosvenor Myer, 'Well Read in Shakespeare', in Valerie Grosvenor Myer (ed.), *Samuel Richardson: Passion and Prudence* (London: Vision, 1986), pp. 126–32; and Adam Rounce, 'Eighteenth-Century Responses to Dryden's *Fables*', *Translation and Literature*, 16 (1) (2007) 29–52 (p. 38).

11 Samuel Richardson, *Selected Letters*, ed. John Carroll (Oxford: Clarendon Press, 1964), p. 160; compare Jonathan Swift, *A Tale of a Tub and Other Works*, ed. Marcus Walsh (Cambridge: Cambridge University Press, 2010), p. 96: 'we of this age have discovered a shorter, and more prudent method, to become scholars and wits, without the fatigue of reading or of thinking'; for recent work on anthologies in the eighteenth century, see, for instance, Price, *The Anthology and the Rise of the Novel*, and Daniel Cook, 'Authors Unformed: Reading "Beauties" in the Eighteenth Century', *Philological Quarterly*, 89 (2–3) (2010): 283–309.

12 See William Empson, *Seven Types of Ambiguity* (London: The Hogarth Press, 1984), p. 213.

13 Jacqueline Rose, *The Haunting of Sylvia Plath* (London: Virago, 1991), pp. 50, 59.

14 Thomas Otway, *Venice Preserv'd*, ed. Malcolm Kelsall (London: Edward Arnold, 1969), V.iv.2–16.

15 On Ophelia in the period, see Jean I. Marsden, *Fatal Desire: Women, Sexuality, and the English Stage, 1660–1720* (Ithaca, NY: Cornell University Press, 2006), p. 90; for Clarissa as 'Ophelia-like', see Rita Goldberg, *Sex and Enlightenment: Women in Richardson and Diderot* (Cambridge: Cambridge University Press, 1984), p. 120.

16 Connaughton, 'Richardson's Familiar Quotations', p. 188.

17 Benjamin, *The Origin of German Tragic Drama*, p. 28.

92 Samuel Richardson and the theory of tragedy

18 In the play these lines refer not only to 'that day's guilt' but to 'this day's guilt and falsehood' (Otway, *Venice Preserv'd*, IV.ii.108); the contraction appears in Edward Bysshe, *The Art of English Poetry*, 2 vols. (London, 1718) vol. I, p. 66.
19 Otway, *Venice Preserv'd*, II.iii.118, 119.
20 Otway, *Venice Preserv'd*, IV.i.1–3. For the relevant suggestion that 'Belvedira balances Pierre as tempter to Jaffeir', see Marsden, *Fatal Desire*, p. 80.
21 Otway, *Venice Preserv'd*, I.i.315, 347. Belvedira seems to rework Shakespeare's Cleopatra in *Antony and Cleopatra* to her own attendants: 'do not speak to me. Lead me to my chamber' (II.v.120).
22 Otway, *Venice Preserv'd*, V.iv.315.
23 See John Milton, *The Complete Poems*, ed. B. A. Wright (London: J. M. Dent & Sons, 1980), pp. 159, 5, 42, 443; for a useful account of the muse motif in poetry at mid-century, see John E. Sitter, 'Mother, Memory, Muse and Poetry after Pope', *ELH*, 44 (2) (1977): 312–36.
24 Joseph Warton, 'The Enthusiast: or The Lover of Nature' in *The New Oxford Book of Eighteenth-Century Verse*, ed. Roger Lonsdale (Oxford: Oxford University Press, 1984), pp. 389–90 (p. 389).
25 Edward Young, *Night Thoughts*, ed. Stephen Cornford (Cambridge: Cambridge University Press, 1989), p. 38.
26 William Collins, 'Ode to Evening' in *The New Oxford Book of Eighteenth-Century Verse*, pp. 381–2 (p. 382).
27 See George T. Wright, 'Hendiadys in Hamlet', *PMLA*, 96 (2) (1981): 168–93.
28 See Standish Henning, 'Branding Harlots on the Brow', *Shakespeare Quarterly*, 51 (1) (2000): 86–9.
29 For another account of the difficulty of using Shakespeare quotation to talk about virginity in the eighteenth century, see J. A. Smith, 'Telling Love: *Twelfth Night* in Samuel Richardson, Teresia Constantia Phillips, and William Blake', *Studies in Philology*, 121 (1) (2015): 194–212.
30 Lacan, *The Ethics of Psychoanalysis*, p. 239.
31 Benjamin, *The Origin of German Tragic Drama*, p. 218.
32 See Bysshe, *The Art of English Poetry*, vol. I, p. 258.
33 Abraham Cowley, 'The Despair', in *The Collected Works of Abraham Cowley*, ed. Thomas O. Calhoun and others, 6 vols. (Newark, Del.: University of Delaware Press, 1993), vol. II.1, pp. 43–4.

34 Andrew Marvell, 'A Dialogue Between the Soul and Body' in *The Complete Poems*, ed. Elizabeth Story Donno (London: Penguin, 2005), pp. 103–4 (p. 104).
35 Richardson, *Selected Letters*, p. 160; for Cowley's precarious reputation in the eighteenth century and comment on Richardson's admiration for him, see Jean Loiseau, *Abraham Cowley's Reputation in England* (Paris: Henri Didier, 1931), pp. 59–62, 66.
36 Samuel Johnson, 'Life of Cowley', in Roger Lonsdale and John Mullen (eds), *The Lives of the Poets: A Selection* (Oxford: Oxford University Press, 2009), pp. 5–53 (p. 25).
37 Bysshe, *The Art of English Poetry*, vol. I, p. 112.
38 Benjamin, *The Origin of German Tragic Drama*, p. 179.
39 Thomas Mann, *Doctor Faustus*, trans. H. T. Lowe-Porter (Harmondsworth: Penguin, 1973), p. 466; and Jeremy Tambling, 'Opera and Novel Ending Together: *Die Meistersinger* and *Doktor Faustus*', *Forum for Modern Language Studies*, 48 (2) (2012): 208–21 (p. 212).
40 Johnson, 'Life of Cowley', p. 16.
41 Benjamin, *The Origin of German Tragic Drama*, p. 140.

3

The rape of Clarissa is marked by the collapse of her discourse into a strange and exploratory constellation of fragments, but it affects Lovelace in an at least momentarily similar way. When he first meets with Clarissa after the rape, Lovelace finds himself reduced to an uncharacteristic 'hesitating effort to speak':

> She entered with such dignity in her manner, as struck me with great awe, and prepared me for the poor figure I made in the subsequent conversation.
> [...]
> By my soul, Belford, my whole frame was shaken: for not only her looks, and her action, but her voice, so solemn, was inexpressibly affecting: and then my cursed guilt, and her innocence and merit, and rank, and superiority of talents, all stared me at that instant in the face so formidably, that my present account, to which she unexpectedly called me, seemed, as I then thought, to resemble that general one to which we are told we shall be summoned, when our conscience shall be our accuser.
> [...]
> My dear – my love – I – I – I never – no never – lips trembling, limbs quaking, voice inward, hesitating, broken – Never surely did miscreant look so *like* a miscreant! [...] What – what-a – what – has been done – I, I, I – cannot but say – must own – must confess – hem – hem – is not right – is not what should have been – But-a – but – but – I am truly – truly – sorry for it – Upon my soul I am – And – and – will do all – do everything – do what – whatever is incumbent upon me – all

that you – that you – that you shall require, to make you amends! – (C 899–901)

The usually suave Lovelace collapses into 'broken sentences and confusion' (C 901) when faced with Clarissa, who, far from being brought low by the rape strikes Lovelace in this moment as a figure of incontestable power. She has something of what Lacan calls 'the splendour of Antigone', a beauty bordering on the destructive and obscene because encountered in too unmediated a form ('all stared me at that instant in the face so formidably') and such that Lovelace feels hurried to the point of making an account of himself at the apocalypse itself. The effect of this encounter with Clarissa is both traumatic and debilitating. 'She made me shudder', he says a little later, 'she is the only *woman* in the world who could have shocked and disturbed me as she has done – So we are upon a foot in that respect ... I can neither think nor write!' (C 911).

Part of what is disturbing about all this for Lovelace is that it represents the emergence of a new pattern of 'the things he expects to happen', as Judith Wilt puts it, *not happening*.[1] In this respect, perhaps the most important of the received notions cultivated in the first volumes of the book is the rakish maxim '*once subdued ... always subdued*' because it proves to be the basis of just this kind of disappointed anticipation. Lovelace's stuttered apology to Clarissa includes the promise to do all 'that you shall require, to make you amends', as if the wrong of the rape could be righted and Clarissa and he could emerge from it with some sort of relationship intact. Famously, he was scarcely alone in this, as a sizeable part of Richardson's real-life readership continued until fairly late in the proceedings to petition for just such a making of amends. But Clarissa's behaviour after the rape represents an absolute refusal to behave in accordance with the expectation that she will forgive Lovelace and, 'subdued', remain with him. This refusal – made in the face of the expectations and advice of virtually every character in the book and plenty of people outside it – is Clarissa's tragic commitment: a decision to side with destruction rather than become complicit with a false wholeness performed in accordance with Lovelace and his culture's corrupted received notions.

Lovelace's first faltering attempt to face Clarissa after the rape introduces three motifs that will take on increasing importance in the final phase of the novel. First, it produces a set piece that the novel will return to several times: Lovelace petitioning Clarissa for forgiveness. Second, it shows Lovelace in a state where he can 'neither think nor write', nor indeed effectively speak, and so at a point where the available practices of representation seem to be breaking down. And third, in Lovelace's emphasis on the encounter with Clarissa as one of *insufficient mediation*, it gestures obliquely towards the conventional preoccupation in the epistolary novel with its own status as a collection of mediating documents. The argument of this chapter is that these three motifs – the importance of mediation, the inability to write and the petition for forgiveness – are structurally related to each other in a way that in turn elucidates the significance of Clarissa's behaviour here to the novel's tragedy.

I begin this chapter by arguing that the key to understanding this section of the novel is to realise its renewed emphasis on the mediated status of the epistolary novel. As Thomas Keymer has remarked, the plot of every epistolary novel is ghosted by a 'second story ... a story of characters at writing-desks'.[2] With reference to a section of *Sir Charles Grandison* with revealing similarities to this part of *Clarissa*, I begin by arguing that Richardson seems to become more interested in such second stories when things are getting particularly fraught in the main 'first' one.

Next, I consider the relationship between Clarissa's mad papers and Lovelace's claim that he is unable to speak, write or think effectively on encountering Clarissa after the rape. While we have seen that the mad papers may be examined for what they tell us about Clarissa's psychology after the rape, it has less often been noticed that as far as the 'second story' of the epistolary novel is concerned, she did not strictly speaking write them. As they are encountered by the reader of Richardson's novel, the mad papers are supposed to be a transcription of something Clarissa has written, copied into one of Lovelace's letters to Belford. Given the amount of transcription that goes on in Richardson's novels generally, this might not stand out as significant but for the fact that Richardson goes to quite odd lengths in providing his reader with hints of what is supposed to have gone on with the papers during this transcription. If we follow these hints, we see that his attempt at copying out Clarissa's words seems to be interrupted by his own debilitating inhibitions in a similar way to his other efforts to speak, write and think at this point in the novel. As something of Clarissa's psychology can be traced at the level of the mad papers' content, something of Lovelace's here can be traced at the level of the mediations of the epistolary form.

After the rape, Lovelace's behaviour is dominated by his desire to have Clarissa forgive him, and for a while it looks as if his inability to speak, write, think or transcribe effectively will stay with him for as long as she refuses to do so. In this respect – or so I want to show – the language, logic and metaphors of Richardson's representation of Lovelace after the rape have a surprising amount in common with the work of Melanie Klein and the British 'object relations' school of psychoanalysis. Turning to Klein in the third section of the chapter, I consider the possibility that Richardson represents in Lovelace a similar fantasy of healing, repair and making reparation to the other to that found in Kleinian therapy and – in the chapter's final section – argue that Richardson demonstrates in Clarissa's refusal to comply with this project the tragic limit point of such thinking.

I

We have already seen how *Clarissa* quietly draws attention to the way the 'instantaneous descriptions and reflections' (C 35) Richardson claimed to be the great advantage of the epistolary novel tend to be undermined by the form's decidedly non-instantaneous and mediated dependence on the transportation and exchange of physical material letters. Like *Clarissa*, *Sir Charles Grandison* has at its centre an instance of female madness: in this case the melancholy of Clementina, which forms part of the long account of Sir Charles's youthful travels in Italy. As in *Clarissa*, the difficulty of narrating this appears to activate a peculiar self-consciousness within the epistolary form itself. Examination of this section of *Sir Charles Grandison* suggests how such moments cause what Keymer calls the 'second story' of how the epistolary text is supposed to have been brought together to make itself known.

The narrative of Clementina's madness comes into the novel in a phase that veers between emphasising openness and emphasising secrecy. Openness characterises the sentimental culture that is emerging between Sir Charles, Charlotte Grandison and Harriet Byron, in which they allow each other to read their respective correspondences for the sake of the moral and emotional education this is supposed to provide.[3] Secrecy, meanwhile, haunts Harriet's growing conviction that Sir Charles has a secret love interest and that she in turn is going to have to keep her growing infatuation with him a secret (SCG II, 70–2, 89). Sir Charles describes his female interlocutors as 'the most frank and open-hearted young ladies in the world' (SCG II, 111), adding that 'my heart is opened by the frankness of yours' (115). This prompts him to tell the story of how he was employed as a tutor by an aristocratic family in Italy, how he and the daughter Clementina came close to marriage, but then how – the family demanding his conversion to Catholicism – the marriage fell through and Clementina collapsed into melancholy. Thus far, the novel has placed a good deal of emphasis on Sir Charles's reluctance to reveal all this – he refers to it 'as the affair which, of all others, has most embarrassed me' (SCG II, 118) – and yet precisely at the moment that is dramatically set up as the point of its final disclosure, the story gets mixed up in a surprisingly convoluted series of mediations.

The first mediation comes in the form of Sir Charles's confidant, the Revd Dr Bartlett. On preparing to tell the story of Clementina, Sir Charles describes his relationship with the older man, going back to the time of his Italian travels:

> He and I have corresponded for years with an intimacy that has few examples between a youth and a man in advanced life. And here let me own the advantages I have received from his condescension; for I have found the following questions often occur to me, and to be of the highest service in the conduct of my life – 'What account shall I give of this to Dr Bartlett?' – Or, 'Shall I be an hypocrite, and only inform him of the best, and meanly conceal from him the worst?' (SCG II, 116)

The period's usual sentimental connection between emotional honesty and moral goodness becomes unusually literal in the young Charles's correspondence. Not only is Dr Bartlett a sound and welcome judge of Charles's conduct, but the mere existence of their correspondence works to determine that conduct in advance, since Charles is always anticipating how his actions will appear when he is inevitably called to describe them in his letters. 'Thus, Madam, was Dr Bartlett in the place of a second conscience to me', Sir Charles continues, 'and many a good thing did I do, many a bad one avoid, for having set up such a monitor over my conduct' (SCG II, 116). Richardson tends to represent letter-writing as a form lending itself to an idealised candour, where the whole of a person's emotional life can be expressed with minimum interruption. But, at the same time, this pure expression of personhood is represented as taking place under the shadow of some 'other': here the 'second conscience' of the interlocutor.

A similar disjunction appears in a later text in the Richardsonian epistolary tradition. Mary Hays' preface to her *Memoirs of Emma Courtney* (1796) addresses 'those readers' of the fictional Emma's writings 'who feel inclined to judge with severity the extravagance and eccentricity of her conduct', urging them to 'look into their own hearts', where they may find a 'record, traced by an accusing spirit, to soften the asperity of their censure'.[4] Mary Jacobus has situated these remarks within 'the Enlightenment ideal of shared intimacy and transparent communication' to which Hays – as part of the circle of William Godwin and Mary Wollstonecraft – was among the more active English contributors. 'The letter is not so much a means of overcoming separation', Jacobus suggests, 'as an imaginary form of thought-transference capable of abolishing difference altogether'.[5] The abolishment of difference aspired to in the letters between the young Charles and Dr Bartlett in *Sir Charles Grandison* is extended to the readers of *Memoirs of Emma Courtney*, who are now compelled to recognise that Emma's 'extravagance and eccentricity' are also their own. But whether it takes the form of a 'second conscience' or an 'accusing spirit', such morally idealised forms of transparency can only be regulated by appeal to some mysteriously externalised supplementary other.

The description of Dr Bartlett's relationship to Sir Charles positions him precariously between being the agent of unmediated exposure and openness and the figure who proves that there can be no such openness without some sort of interrupting mediation. But this is only the start of it. As Sir Charles prepares to explain the story of Clementina to Harriet, he proposes a slightly odd arrangement. 'I do not intend, madam, to trouble you with an history of all that part of my life', he says, 'after this entrance into it, Dr Bartlett shall be at liberty to satisfy your curiosity in a more *particular* manner' (SCG II, 116). What this means is that Sir Charles will actually give the promised unvarnished account of the miserable episode only in the form of a précis. That done, Dr Bartlett will take over, and Sir Charles will, he says, 'beg of him to let you see anything you shall wish to see, in the free and unreserved correspondence we have held' (SCG II, 131). This takes the form of thirteen long letters to Harriet from Dr Bartlett, who, as Leah Price puts it, is turned into 'a sort of scribal publisher who strings together snippets from Grandison's letters with third-person plot summaries' so that the young Charles's letters 'come to be edited as thoroughly as any published correspondence'.[6] Certainly, Dr Bartlett's interventions in the story go well beyond the 'few lines here and there, by way of connexion' (SCG II, 136–7) he initially licenses himself to add. And Richardson even adds another mediating hand to the equation: the task is to be shared with Dr Bartlett's nephew, 'transcribing', says Harriet, 'the passages that will enable him to perform the task he has so kindly undertaken' (SCG II, 136).

Despite the surprisingly laboured editorial project he is engaged in, Dr Bartlett's involvement in telling the story of Clementina is still being couched in the language of spontaneous 'free and unreserved' communication (SCG II, 131). But while his guardianship of Sir Charles's archive of letters may allow him to produce evidence of what the young Charles was writing at the time, it can't escape our notice that his role also absolves Sir Charles of much of the painful duty of explaining what went on himself. Several times in his comparatively brief initial account, Sir Charles leaves matters unelaborated, referring Harriet – and so the novel's reader – to Dr Bartlett instead (SCG II, 118, 125, 128). And even Harriet, once both Sir Charles and Dr Bartlett's versions of the story have been told, remarks that 'it will be no wonder to us now, that Sir Charles was not solicitous to make known a situation so embarrassing to himself, and so much involved in clouds and uncertainty' (SCG II, 258).

The mass of mediations does not end here, however, because this messy combination of the present Sir Charles's voice, the young Charles's edited words, Dr Bartlett's editorial summaries and his nephew's transcriptions only finds its place in the archive of the novel through the lens of Harriet. During Sir Charles's initial schematic account, Harriet begins to feel faint and accuses herself of '*causelessly* laying my disorder on his story' (SCG II, 119). This is a revealing moment because it signals how she is still less a neutral conduit for the story of Clementina's madness than Sir Charles and Dr Bartlett. After reading Dr Bartlett's anthology-letters, she forwards them successively to her main correspondent, Lucy Selby, accompanied by her own fraught reflections on the significance of the developments they describe for her own prospects with Sir Charles. Harriet fears at one point that Sir Charles has deliberately counselled Dr Bartlett to represent the history of his relationship with Clementina in such a way as to 'check any hopes that I might entertain, before they had too strongly taken hold of my foolish heart' (SCG II, 162). But she herself has already allowed present concerns to influence the representation of the past when she admits to being 'half guilty of an affectation' (SCG II, 135) in especially asking Dr Bartlett to include letters in his account in which she has no interest, in the hope they will cover over her preoccupation with those directly concerned with Charles's feelings for Clementina.

The difficult topic of the madness of Clementina is a major test case for the ethics of candid openness *Sir Charles Grandison* seems to have been written to promote. It is strange then, that at this very moment the novel finds it necessary to fall back on a weirdly complicated series of mediating commentaries and editorial apparatuses. These mediating delays and belated deferrals call into question the instantaneousness of Richardson's treasured 'instantaneous descriptions' in letters once again, but, more than this, Harriet's situation also shows how such descriptions actually refuse to stay put in their historical 'instant', rather continuing to roguishly *instantiate* themselves on those who read or hear them subsequently. While Sir Charles and Dr Bartlett work to produce an accurate archive of what happened with Clementina at the time of Charles's travels, Harriet is creating a striking visualisation of how present those disturbing events are becoming for her. In another of Richardson's visually unusual experimentations with the novelistic page, she appends to Dr Bartlett's first anthology-letter two columns detailing 'a parallel between our two cases' (SCG II, 158), comparing the situation of Clementina with her own.

II

We have noted that recent readings of *Clarissa* have stressed how it 'periodically strays from its visual uniformity as a printed book in order to approximate graphically the look of original letters'.[7] But the supposed meetings of manuscript and print created in *Clarissa*'s block-printed signatures, marginal indexing hands and fold-out musical score do not elide the question of *which letters* it is the book is supposed to be approximating. The build-up of transcriptions, abridgements and annotations that the exchange of letters concerning Charles and Clementina in *Sir Charles Grandison* provokes – and the opportunities for subtle manipulation we have seen this afford – serves to draw attention to the way that the specific copies of the letters that we are supposed to imagine have become copy texts for the printed novel have material implications for how they are received: both by the novel's readers and by its characters. While this long middle section of *Sir Charles Grandison* is ostensibly about the young Charles and the madness of Clementina, a considerable amount of detail about Harriet's feelings for Sir Charles is revealed in her responses to Dr Bartlett's transcriptions of the relevant letters. Indeed, this is an editorial process that Harriet admits to having tried to influence, as well as to suspecting Sir Charles of having done the same. If such mediating filters make themselves especially known around the point of *Sir Charles Grandison*'s main representation of female madness, then they certainly do the same around the analogous point in *Clarissa*. In Chapter 2, I examined in detail the implications of some specific parts of Clarissa's mad papers for the rest of the novel, but here I want to demonstrate that Richardson seems just as invested in hinting at how they are supposed have got into the novel in the first place.

Between the rape of Clarissa and Lovelace's traumatised subsequent meeting with her, Clarissa has written Lovelace a letter, which, when finished, she glances back over, adding despondently that 'it is not fit for anyone to see, so far as I have been able to re-peruse it: but my head will not hold, I doubt, to go through it all' (C 896). By the time we get to read it, we have already seen something of Lovelace's response to it, when it is brought to him by the servant Dorcas in the same bundle as the 'scraps and fragments' (C 889) that constitute the mad papers a few pages earlier. As these first writings of Clarissa after the rape are delivered to Lovelace, their arrival interrupts him attempting to write to Belford, and it is in the form of a transcription within this letter that Clarissa's mad writings are to actually come into the novel. Just as *Sir Charles Grandison* does not allow its reader access to Clementina's madness except through a mesh of transcriptions, annotations and commentary, Clarissa's famous breakdown after the rape only reaches the reader of *Clarissa* in the form of a highly unusual and collaboratively written letter signed, peculiarly enough, by Lovelace.

Lovelace's letter begins with a discordantly comic aside about having heard that Belford has fallen while riding – 'what a narrow escape thou hadst with thy neck' – prompting Lovelace to caution that 'a rake's neck is always in danger, if not from the hangman, from his own horse' (C 888). There are other hangings in Richardson: in the first edition of *Pamela*, Pamela has seen a public execution, although it is among the ungenteel details Richardson embarrassedly suppressed in subsequent editions.[8] In *Clarissa* itself, it is one of the ghosts that shadows the Harlowe family that a man is supposed to have been found hanging on their grounds shortly before Clarissa's birth (C 164). In Lovelace's case, the reference is an associative jump supplying a witticism – whether comically or tragically, a rake is always prone to break his neck – but this jumping between two kinds of neck breaking sets up a pattern that continues to code the development of the letter. The next thing Lovelace discusses is his own disinclination to write: 'how can I think it in my *power* to divert, when my subject is not pleasing to myself'. Comparing himself to Julius Caesar, Lovelace next swings from considering the melancholy of having achieved everything he had set out to, to interrupting himself with the thought that having resorted to rape he has achieved nothing at all: 'why say I *completed*? when the *will*, the *consent*, is wanting'. Finally, he turns to describe Clarissa's manic state, and the fact that whereas he is struggling to write, she has begun to write once more. During the considerations that follow, Lovelace is twice interrupted by his servant, Dorcas, reporting back from Clarissa's chamber:

Last night, for the first time since Monday last, she got to her pen and ink: but she pursues her writing with such eagerness and hurry, as show too evidently her discomposure.

I hope, however, that this employment will help to calm her spirits.

* *

Just now Dorcas tells me that what she writes she tears, and throws the paper in fragments under the table, either as not knowing what she does, or disliking it: then gets up, wrings her hands, weeps, and shifts her seat all round the room: then returns to her table, sits down, and writes again.

* *

ONE odd letter, as I may call it, Dorcas has this moment given me from her – *Carry this*, said she, *to the vilest of men*. (C 889)

At first Lovelace hopes that Clarissa's return to writing will prove therapeutic, an 'employment ... to calm her spirits', but instead he finds that the product of Clarissa's writing session is the odd letter that we will later learn she has not even been able to 're-peruse' herself, along with the 'scraps and fragments' of the mad papers.

It is worth pausing over the remarkable kind of prose poetry Richardson is creating here: certainly, it cannot be described as straightforwardly representational or realistic. Taken in isolation, Lovelace's remarks may be innocuous enough, but it is as if a caesural strain or impulse to cut things off rattles through the letter when taken as a whole, producing a piece of writing founded on a metonymic series of breakages. Belford's neck becomes that of an imagined hanged rake, and Lovelace's halting reluctance to write tumbles into his contradicting himself over the question of whether, in turn, the seduction has been left incomplete by the rape. Subsequently, Dorcas interrupting Lovelace's writing by coming into the room transmogrifies into Clarissa's interruptions of herself as she tears her letters apart and begins again. In the previous chapter I suggested that Lovelace's totemic phrase 'I can go no farther' (C 883) and the accompanying caesural absence where narration of the rape might be mark a shift in the novel where the power of the old received notions to predict how situations will turn out is starting to slip. We saw at the start of this chapter meanwhile that when Lovelace finally meets with Clarissa again after the rape, he is overcome by an analogously fragmented inability to communicate. Between these moments, Lovelace's letter containing the mad papers presents a kind of crisis zone where everything – human bodies and lines of thought, seductions and pieces of paper – is toppled into the same pulsing series of breakages.

But there is more. As Lovelace settles down to transcribe Clarissa's first 'odd letter' for Belford, this familiar activity too joins the series of breakages and unfinished acts his letter has already set up. Lovelace says of Clarissa's odd letter that he 'sat down, intending (though 'tis pretty long) to give thee a copy of it: but, for my life, I cannot; 'tis so extravagant. And the original is too much an original to let it go out of my hands' (C 889). Unable to copy Clarissa's letter, Lovelace turns instead to the mad papers:

> Some of the scraps and fragments, as either torn through, or flung aside, I will copy for the novelty of the thing, and to show thee how her mind works now in a whimsical way … Dorcas thinks her lady will ask for them: so wishes to have them lay again under her table. (C 889)

These comments seem overdetermined in their antithetical impulses to dismiss as well as to elevate, to discard as well as preserve. Clarissa's letter is too odd to copy but 'too much an original' to hazard to the vagaries of the post. The mad papers meanwhile have been flung aside by Clarissa and are treated dismissively – 'for the novelty of the thing' – by Lovelace, and yet the originals of these too must be preserved, returned to the strange archive Clarissa is forming underneath her table.

Lovelace's pose of indifference is not sustained. After transcribing Paper I, the mad paper most recognisable as a draft of a letter to Anna Howe, Lovelace abandons his role as Clarissa's copyist in a state of frustration:

> Plague on it! I can write no more of this eloquent nonsense myself; which rather shows a raised, than a quenched

imagination: but Dorcas shall transcribe the others in separate papers, as written by the whimsical charmer: and some time hence, when all is over, and I can better bear to read them, I may ask thee for a sight of them. Preserve them therefore; for we often look back with pleasure even upon the heaviest griefs, when the cause of them is removed. (C 890)

Responsibility for copying the mad papers into Lovelace's letter falls to Dorcas, and despite Lovelace's determination to have them included in the letter, there is every possibility that he has never substantially read them himself. The copying done, Lovelace claims to have 'just skimmed over these transcriptions' (C 894), and, while Belford will later refer to having 'very often since most seriously reflected upon' Clarissa's 'papers written in her delirium', he claims that Lovelace has 'perhaps ... never thought of [them] since' (C 969). The odd letter Lovelace initially refused to include meanwhile is also belatedly transcribed by Dorcas ('the paper, thou'lt see, is blistered with the tears even of the hardened transcriber' [C 896]): 'I cannot', Lovelace says, 'the reading of it affected me ten times more than the severest reproaches of a regular mind' (C 894).

Lovelace's inability to copy out the 'eloquent nonsense' of Clarissa's writing without Dorcas's assistance positions those writings rather strangely as far as the novel is concerned. Like *Sir Charles Grandison*'s letters concerning Clementina's madness, they arrive in the archive of the novel only after undertaking a considerably complicated scene of mediation. But whereas Harriet notes that it is at least possible that such mediation could lead to manipulation by either Sir Charles or herself, here the figure organising the copying can barely even stand to read the texts in the first place. Instead of facing the violently new forms of quotation I have suggested the mad papers bring into the novel, Lovelace retreats into the old received notions with a reassuringly sententious maxim: 'we often look back with pleasure even upon the heaviest griefs, when the cause of them is removed'. This is a variation on a famous maxim found – for one – in Dante, and is pretty staggering in its inadequacy to the situation it is being applied to.⁹ It is not the case that the mad papers could be simply preserved, put to one side and enjoyed with disinterested 'pleasure' when the present unhappiness has passed. Instead, Lovelace's retreat into received notions should be taken as yet more evidence for how these writings have defeated him. While the content of the mad papers may be an extremely suggestive account of the effect the rape has had on Clarissa at the level of the main plot, it is at this level of the practices of mediation the epistolary form makes us aware of at its margins, that the rape's effect on Lovelace is being articulated.

III

By way of a kind of feedback loop, the effect Clarissa's writings have on Lovelace in turn influences the material form they are supposed to take in the novel. The offending originals are who knows where, and a printed approximation of the stuttering multi-authored copy is all we get to see. But why should Richardson's first representation of Lovelace's traumatised response take the specific form of an inability to write in Clarissa's words? An answer can be found by way of a surprising conjunction of Richardson's work with that of the Austrian-British psychoanalyst Melanie Klein. In Kleinian psychoanalysis, the stability of our identities is contingent on our relations with the objects around us: a constellation that may include loved people, material objects, body parts or even abstract ideas. From childhood, our relations with these objects are decided on the plane of unconscious fantasy, which takes the principal forms of 'introjection' – imagining one has taken the object safely inside oneself – and 'projection' – imposing one's feelings of aggression onto the object from outside. These fantasises are omnipotent, Klein argues, in the sense that Freud had given the word in the 'Rat Man' analysis, where he refers to the analysand's anxiety that his most outlandish imaginings may escape to exert themselves on reality as 'the omnipotence of thoughts'.[10] We all have our 'good objects', those on which we depend for our mental consistency, and for Klein the prototype for this object is the figure of the mother. But there is also a 'primary sadism' which causes us to invidiously project violent fantasises onto our objects. In 'Love, Guilt and Reparation' (1937), Klein describes a child imagining the destruction of his mother, only to end up fearing that through the omnipotence of his fantasises he has done her permanent damage:

> If the baby has, in his aggressive phantasies, injured his mother by biting and tearing her up, he may soon build up phantasies that he is putting the bits together again and repairing her. This, however, does not quite do away with his fears of having destroyed the object which, as we know, is the one whom he loves and needs most, and on whom he is entirely dependent.

Before the good object can be successfully introjected once more as the anchor of the child's subjectivity he must make reparation in his fantasy, returning her to her earlier 'goodness'. But this work of reparation which we are all more or less constantly performing threatens to be suspended by two psychological states or 'positions' we are liable to take on when the damaged object is before us. The first is the 'paranoid-schizoid position', an aggressive guarding of the ego from what is now perceived as malicious in the broken pieces of the damaged object, now thought of as 'bad'; and the second is the 'depressive position' which is a state of debilitation that fears that its attempts at making reparation are doomed to be hopeless.[11]

The Kleinian provocation that we must negotiate the twin perils of paranoid-schizoid aggressiveness and morbid depressive inaction through creative acts of reparation has meant that, probably more than any other area of psychoanalytic enquiry, Kleinian psychoanalysis has lent itself to the explicit defence of the moral and reparative value of writing and the arts.[12] Marion Milner, whose psychoanalytic training was supervised by Klein and who analysed Klein's grandson, places drawing, painting and the overcoming of resistances to creativity at the centre of her accounts of analysis in *On Not Being Able to Paint* (1950) and *The Hands of the Living God* (1969).[13] The educationalist David Holbrook, meanwhile, makes a curious synthesis of Leavisite literary criticism and Kleinian analysis in *The Quest for Love* (1965), which takes Chaucer, Shakespeare and D. H. Lawrence as approximations of the Kleinian argument of the psychological necessity of making reparation in order to see the world as good and creative.[14] Holbrook had given a practical application to this argument in his earlier account of trying to teach deprived lower-stream pupils in secondary modern schools in *English for the Rejected* (1964), which equates the child's developing literacy taught through creative writing with a movement towards a 'positive sense of his own goodness, and a positive attitude to life'.[15]

The psychological interpretation of *Clarissa* all this invites is this: Lovelace's inability to transcribe Clarissa's writings and subsequent inability to speak or think properly when he encounters her in person are attributable to what Klein would call 'his fears of having destroyed the object'. Much as Holbrook thought his pupils were impeded in developing their reading and writing by an unconscious sense of having caused too much damage to the world around them, Lovelace has lost his capacity to write precisely in so far as he perceives that he has damaged the good object, Clarissa, beyond all reparation.[16] Lovelace's discussions of the mad papers, and the mad papers themselves, actually tend towards the very imagery and terminology Klein adopts when discussing the paranoid-schizoid position, which she describes as the fantasy that the disintegrated object destroyed by the subject's aggression has returned as 'a multitude of persecutors, since each piece is growing again into a persecutor'.[17] 'I know I am furnishing thee with new weapons against myself', Lovelace writes to Belford as he begins to attempt the transcription, 'but spare thy comments. My own reflections render them needless' (C 889). While Lovelace is conscious of having caused the damage that has produced the fragmentary papers in the first place, he experiences the fragments as 'new weapons' in themselves, 'growing again into a persecutor', as Klein would put it. The idea could have been taken from Clarissa herself. Paper I, the only one of the mad papers actually transcribed by Lovelace, refers to her own thoughts and internal voices as just such 'bad object' persecutors: 'thought, and grief, and confusion ... crowding so thick upon me; *one* would be first, *another* would be first, *all* would be first' (C 890).

These similarities at the level of imagery are matched by similarities at the level of terminology. As much as it is a keyword for Klein, 'reparation' becomes one for Richardson and is increasingly used in the final volumes to refer to Lovelace's attempts to make amends with Clarissa, to have her forgive and finally marry him. If the strange abortive rhythms that overtake the novel after the rape are announced by a combination of Clarissa's mad writing and Lovelace's debilitating failure to write at all, then we can start to see the latter as an indication of the fact that Lovelace will actually never be allowed to make reparation. Lovelace refers to his overtures of forgiveness and marriage to Clarissa as an 'endeavour to persuade her to consent to the reparation of her own honour' (C 959), later worrying that 'according to her own notions ... I have injured her beyond reparation, although I were to make her the best of husbands' (C 1039). Advising Belford in his capacity as Lovelace's petitioner for Clarissa's forgiveness, Lovelace says, 'I think thou hadst better ... forbear to urge her on the subject of accepting the reparation I offer, lest the continual teasing of her to forgive me should but strengthen her in her denials of forgiveness' (C 1143). As well as the ten or so other uses of the word in similar contexts we could cite here, Richardson seems to have been sufficiently preoccupied with it that he added yet more examples to the revised third edition.[18] In one case, the example of Belford's reflection on the death of the libertine Belton – 'I will endeavour ... to make some atonement, as near to restitution or reparation as is possible, to those I have wronged' (3C VI, 270) – the words 'or reparation' are the only change Richardson made to the passage.

Lovelace's wish to make reparation by having Clarissa forgive him and consent to marriage would not necessarily have seemed strange in the eighteenth century. On the contrary, it reflects wider cultural assumptions that the damage perceived to be done to a woman by consensual or non-consensual premarital sex could be simply repaired and reversed by marriage: assumptions that were also reflected in law. The legal scholar Gwynn Davis has commented on a general tolerance in eighteenth-century law for symbolic reparative gestures that favoured public apology over punitive or material recompense.[19] Discussing the legal status of rape specifically, Frances Ferguson emphasises the long history of the belief that marriage may constitute 'legal recompense for rape', manufacturing in retrospect 'consent to intercourse that was previously lacking'.[20] As Susan Staves points out, marriage was proposed as recompense in place of punishment in several of the cases of rape overseen by Henry Fielding during his time as a magistrate.[21] The Harlowes, indeed, simply reverse that situation when they tell Clarissa that if she is not prepared to bring about 'the reparation of your family dishonour' by marrying Lovelace, she must 'prosecute him at law' (C 1251). Marriage is conceived as an alternative form of reparation, both in the practical sense that it comes as an offer of compensation to the wronged woman, and – as Sandra Macpherson has argued is repeatedly the case in Fielding's fiction – at the level of narrative, in that it transforms a faulty tragic story into a triumphantly comic one.[22]

Lovelace seems to trust in these legal and literary comedies when he remarks that 'MARRIAGE, *with these women … is an atonement for all we can do to them*' (C 1039), but also when he laments of Clarissa, 'oh that she would forgive me! – Would she but generously forgive me, and receive my vows at the altar, at the *instant* of her forgiving me' (C 930). The commitment here is to a specifiable '*instant*' that would have the power to redeem both Clarissa and him simultaneously, bringing into domestic normality and moral clarity a situation which has become decidedly strange and damaged. In Ferguson's reading, Richardson had already flirted with such an idea in his first novel when he allowed Mr B to instantaneously rewrite the history of his relationship with Pamela as just a particularly convoluted but otherwise unobjectionable courtship, his attempted rapes as mere stages in the proposal. As Ferguson puts it, this left Pamela's virtuous resistance open to looking like 'an instrument in a marriage campaign rather than an end in itself'.[23] What is distinctive about Clarissa is that she doesn't believe in any such '*instant*', and this perhaps is the key qualification we need to make to our Kleinian reading of the novel thus far. During his fumbled and abortive attempts to transcribe the mad papers, Lovelace behaves like a model Kleinian analysand, struggling to make reparation to an object he perceives that he has ruined. But as the novel's final instalment proceeds and this struggle is displaced by the text onto his repeated failed attempts to petition Clarissa for forgiveness, it is emphatically Clarissa herself who has become the impediment to reparation being successfully made.

IV

In a meeting with Clarissa subsequent to the traumatic first one we began this chapter with, Lovelace addresses her with a petition for forgiveness which, consistent with the logic of the '*instant*' he imagines could combine marriage with the completion of reparation, is also a marriage proposal:

> This is the last time, my dearest life, that you will ever see me in this posture, on this occasion: and again I kneeled to her – Let me hope that you will be mine next Thursday, your uncle's birthday, if not before. Would to Heaven I had never been a villain! Your indignation is not, cannot be, greater than my remorse – and I took hold of her gown; for she was going from me. (C 929)

The reply comes: 'Be remorse thy portion! – For thy own sake, be remorse thy portion! – I never, never will forgive thee! – I never, never will be thine! – Let me retire! – Why kneelest thou to the wretch whom thou hast so vilely humbled?' Much later, Clarissa will make a considerably qualified gesture towards reneging on this vow to never forgive Lovelace, writing to him that 'religion enjoins me not only to forgive injuries, but to return good for evil … I am now in such a state of mind with regard to you, that I can cheerfully obey its dictates. And accordingly tell you that wherever you go, I wish you happy' (C 1191). Even this prompts Lovelace's wonder that it does not accompany an acceptance of his marriage proposal: 'I have sinned! I repent! I would repair – She forgives my sin! She accepts my repentance! But she won't let me repair!' (C 1208). Clarissa will wait until she is on her deathbed before finally telling Belford that he should 'tell your friend that I forgive him! And I pray to God to forgive him ... pausing, and lifting up her eyes as if praying that He would' (C 1362). Even this, however, gets a rather more impersonal and pernickety rewording when actually addressed to Lovelace: 'I should mistrust my own penitence were I capable of wishing to recompense evil for evil – if, black as your offences have been against me, I could not forgive as I wish to be forgiven' (C 1426).

Clarissa does not forgive, at least not until she is safely out of the way of any possibility of stabilising social relations between Lovelace and her in the manner that eighteenth-century law and much of its fiction would encourage. Anna writes to Clarissa during this phase, applauding her 'resolution not to have this vilest of men' (C 1150) but admits that she, like Lovelace and his family, had initially wanted Clarissa to take the trajectory of accepting reparation: 'to be prevailed upon by the solicitations of *his* friends', albeit 'before you carried your resentments to so great a height'. Now, Anna compliments Clarissa for being 'fixed' in her 'noble resolution', adding that 'I thought it was impossible there could be (however desirable) so noble an instance given by any of our sex, of a passion conquered, when there were so many inducements to give way to it.'

'Fixed' in the face of all 'solicitations' and 'inducements' to the contrary, Clarissa's gesture identifies in the equation of forgiveness, marriage and reparation one of the major received notions examined in the novel, and it is one that she overwhelmingly refuses. Critics have not always taken kindly to how Richardson frames this, and the question has often been raised whether in her vow to 'never, never ...

forgive' and in the rather sinister 'be remorse thy portion', Clarissa lays herself open to the charge of having adopted a position of self-righteous victimhood.[24] In his remarkable interrogation of the concept of forgiveness, Jacques Derrida warns of just such a tendency on the part of the person being petitioned to forgive, especially when forgiveness is only granted 'on the condition that the guilty one repents', a gesture which must always be implicitly 'addressed from the top down', while assuming 'for itself the power of forgiving, be it as victim or in the name of the victim'.[25] But this power dynamic inside the concept of forgiveness also works the other way. In the meeting between Clarissa and Lovelace where she makes her major gesture of refusing his petition for forgiveness, Lovelace's warning that 'this is the last time ... you will ever see me in this posture' (C 929) and even the detail of his taking 'hold of her gown' to prevent her leaving, all indicate that there can also be a measure of power afforded to the person who demands to be forgiven, especially when he gives the impression that the window in which forgiveness could be accepted is a limited one.

For all Richardson's proto-Kleinian imagery, terminology and psychological insight, the ethics of his novel are ultimately profoundly oppositional to hers in that it comes down on the side of an outright refusal of the idea that reparation should be permitted to be made. In this respect, Clarissa's resistance to forgiving Lovelace in any straightforward way brings her markedly close to Derrida's analogously principled wariness of forgiveness as conventionally understood:

> Each time forgiveness is at the service of a finality, be it noble and spiritual (atonement or redemption, reconciliation, salvation), each time that it aims to re-establish a normality (social, national, political, psychological) by a work of mourning, by some therapy or ecology of memory, then the 'forgiveness' is not pure – nor is its concept. Forgiveness is not, it *should not be*, normal, normative, normalising. It should *remain* exceptional and extraordinary, in the face of the impossible: as if it interrupted the ordinary course of historical temporality.[26]

Quite apart from the dubious power games it lends itself to, the problem with forgiveness is that it is too corrective, too economic by its very structure. The 'I forgive you', granted in response to an adequate display of penitence, assumes real or imagined wrongdoing can be straightforwardly paid off, leaving no remainder and returning everything to normal. 'Normal' in deconstruction is precisely the problem, which is why the only forgiveness Derrida could contemplate would be of an absolutely unforgiveable act. This alone would represent a pure and 'extraordinary' forgiveness, 'without condition', capable of avoiding either the murky economic logic of exchange or the reactionary ethics of simply getting everything back to business.

I cannot say that Richardson goes as far down the path as to contemplate such a radically deconstructive concept of forgiveness. But he does get as far as revealing a profound mistrust of the kinds of forgiveness available to Clarissa, except, in the final instance, the dutiful forgiveness of those who have wronged us demanded by Christianity. The expectation comes from all quarters – from Lovelace, his family, and even at one stage from Anna – that Clarissa will comply with the received notion 'once subdued always subdued' and forgive and marry Lovelace in such a way that allows him to make reparation. But Clarissa is no more willing than Derrida to simply return everything to normal once the tragic break has occurred, and this failure of the received notions is registered at the level of the text itself seeming to materially collapse and fail to reproduce itself as we read it. On the contrary, in the manner of Lacan's Antigone, Clarissa's opposition to all kinds of repair extends even to herself. As Lovelace suggests, her ultimate refusal is not only of him but is also of 'the reparation of her own honour' (C 959). The story the text is telling at this point is, from Lovelace's point of view, a model comic and Kleinian one of stultifying inhibition being overcome by eventual reparation being made to the damaged object. But Clarissa's story from here will be something much more difficult indeed.

Notes

1 Schulz and Wilt, 'Lovelace and Impotence', p. 1006.
2 Keymer, *Richardson's Clarissa*, p. 48; see also the observation of Bernard Duyfhuizen, 'Epistolary Narratives of Transmission and Transgression', *Comparative Literature*, 37 (1) (1985): 1–26 (p. 1): 'all epistolary novels contain a double narrative: a narrative of the events and a narrative of the letters that precipitate or report the events'.
3 Margaret Anne Doody observes that whereas characters good and bad frequently find either value, advantage or solace in dissimulation and concealment in *Pamela* and *Clarissa*, *Sir Charles Grandison* places the greatest moral emphasis on an idealised openness; see her 'Identity and Character in *Sir Charles Grandison*', in Margaret Anne Doody and Peter Sabor (eds), *Samuel Richardson: Tercentenary Essay* (Cambridge: Cambridge University Press, 1989), pp. 110–32.
4 Mary Hays, *Memoirs of Miss Emma Courtney*, ed. Eleanor Ty (Oxford: Oxford University Press, 2000), p. 4.
5 Mary Jacobus, *Psychoanalysis and the Scene of Reading: The Clarendon Lectures in English Literature, 1997* (Oxford: Oxford University Press, 1999), p. 208.
6 Price, *The Anthology and the Rise of the Novel*, pp. 33–4.
7 Barchas, *Graphic Design*, p. 131.
8 In the first edition, Pamela responds to another servant's claim that he was only doing his duty in helping Mr B: 'I never saw an execution but once, and then the hangman ask'd the poor creature's pardon, and wip'd his mouth, as you do, and pleaded his duty, and then calmly tuck'd up the criminal' (P 100); in later editions this becomes 'I have heard that the hangman at an execution usually asks the poor creature's pardon, and then pleads his duty, and calmly does his office', see Samuel Richardson, *Pamela; or, Virtue Rewarded*, ed. Margaret Anne Doody and Peter Sabor (London: Penguin, 2003), p. 146.
9 See Dante Alighieri, *Inferno*, ed. and trans. Charles S. Singleton (Princeton, NJ: Princeton University Press, 1970), pp. 54–5: Lovelace's remark reverses Francesca's words in Inferno, 5:121–3, 'nessun maggior dolore / che ricordarsi del tempo felice / ne la miseria' ('there is no greater sorrow than to recall, in wretchedness, the happy time').

10 Sigmund Freud, *Two Case Histories ('Little Hans' and 'The Rat Man')*, ed. and trans. James Strachey (London: Vintage, 2001), p. 23.
11 Melanie Klein, *Love, Guilt and Reparation and Other Works, 1921–1945* (London: Vintage, 1998), pp. 308, 212, 308–9, 265, 269; see also Julia Segal, *Melanie Klein* (London and Thousand Oaks, Calif.: Sage, 2004), pp. 28–33.
12 See Mary Jacobus, *The Poetics of Psychoanalysis: In the Wake of Klein* (Oxford: Oxford University Press, 2005); and Jeremy Tambling, *Literature and Psychoanalysis* (Manchester: Manchester University Press, 2012), pp. 80–3.
13 Marion Milner, *On Not Being Able to Paint* (London: Heinemann, 1950) and *The Hands of the Living God: An Account of a Psycho-analytic Treatment* (London: Hogarth Press, 1969); see also Kelley A. Raab, 'Creativity and Transcendence in the Work of Marion Milner', *American Imago*, 57 (2) (2000): 185–214.
14 David Holbrook, *The Quest for Love* (London: Methuen, 1965); on Holbrook, see Christopher Hilliard, *English as Vocation: The Scrutiny Movement* (Oxford: Oxford University Press, 2012), pp. 124–31.
15 David Holbrook, *English for the Rejected: Training Literacy in the Lower Streams of Secondary Schools* (Cambridge: Cambridge University Press, 1964), p. 70.
16 A psychoanalytic reading that pushed Lovelace's positioning Clarissa as the preeminent Kleinian 'good object', the mother, could refer to his fantasy of feeding at her breast; see Raymond H. Hilliard, '*Clarissa* and Ritual Cannibalism', *PMLA*, 105 (5) (1990), 1083–97 (p. 1089).
17 Klein, *Love, Guilt and Reparation*, p. 272.
18 See C 959, 1035, 1039, 1042, 1171, 1251, 1253, 1281, 1299 and 1331; and 3C VI, 312 and VII, 194.
19 Gwynn Davis, *Making Amends: Mediation and Reparation in Criminal Justice* (London: Routledge, 1992), pp. 3–5; Davis refers in particular to the terms of the anti-poacher 'Black Act' (1723), which enshrined aristocratic sovereignty by allowing for public reparative gestures to be made by trespassers in relation to their landowning 'victims'.
20 Frances Ferguson, 'Rape and the Rise of the Novel', in R. Howard Bloch and Frances Ferguson (eds), *Misogyny, Misandry, and Misanthropy* (Berkeley, Calif.: University of California Press, 1989), pp. 88–112 (p. 92).
21 Susan Staves, 'Fielding and the Comedy of Attempted Rape', in Beth Fowkes Tobin (ed.), *History, Gender, and Eighteenth-Century*

Literature (Athens, Ga.: University of Georgia Press, 1994), pp. 86–112 (p. 106).
22 Macpherson, *Harm's Way*, Chapter 3.
23 Ferguson, 'Rape and the Rise of the Novel', p. 99.
24 For the conclusion that Clarissa's 'eventual forgiveness' is in fact 'fraught with bitterness', see Gerard A. Barker, 'The Complacent Paragon: Exemplary Characterisation in *Clarissa*', *Studies in English Literature, 1500–1900*, 9 (3) (1969): 503–19 (p. 512); for the argument that Clarissa never forgives Lovelace without qualification, see Carol Houlihan Flynn, *Samuel Richardson: A Man of Letters* (Princeton, NJ: Princeton University Press, 1982), pp. 42–5; and for the view that 'Clarissa's insistent forgiveness has an overwhelming ability to damn where it blesses', see Jonathan Loesberg, 'Allegory and Narrative in *Clarissa*', *NOVEL: A Forum on Fiction*, 15 (1) (1981), 39–59 (p. 53); the classic statement about power being adopted in a rhetoric of victimhood is made in Friedrich Nietzsche, *On the Genealogy of Morals*, ed. and trans. Douglas Smith (Oxford: Oxford University Press, 1996), especially pp. 22–5.
25 Jacques Derrida, *On Cosmopolitanism and Forgiveness*, trans. Mark Dooley and Michael Hughes (London and New York: Routledge, 2001), pp. 38, 58.
26 Derrida, *On Cosmopolitanism and Forgiveness*, pp. 31–2.

4

Richardson's death in 1761 was marked in France by Denis Diderot's *Éloge de Richardson*, published the following year. Among extended passages of approbation, Diderot suddenly turns to the following strange fantasy:

> An idea that I have sometimes had when I am thinking about Richardson's works is that I have bought an old château, and, inspecting its various rooms one day, I see in a corner a cupboard which has not been opened for ages, and, breaking it open, I find higgledy-piggledy, the letters of Clarissa and Pamela. When I had read some of them, how eagerly I should have arranged them in the order of their dates! What misery I should have suffered if there had been any gaps in them![1]

Meditating on Richardson's death leads Diderot to imagine an afterlife for the letters represented in his novels as material objects. But how have they come to be carried to and entombed in an old French château? In what distant past does Diderot imagine these events took place? And how have the letters of these two women unknown to each other come to be combined, and, indeed, separated from the letters of the other characters that accompany theirs in their respective novels? *Clarissa* – the novel – exists and is read in *Sir Charles Grandison*, and its characters behave like model Richardsonian readers, mapping the experiences represented in the earlier novel onto their own (see SCG I, 229), but there is no such relationship suggested between *Pamela* and *Clarissa*. It is as if Diderot's show of mourning for Richardson provokes the more drastically melancholic impulse in him to reduce the oeuvre he praises to its mere constituent rubble: a disordered partial narration of two women's lives. But at the same time there is another dimension to the fantasy. Perhaps it befits the man who was at this point struggling to publish the *Encyclopédie* that the response he imagines having to such a chaotic pile of texts is to bring it into order, arranging the letters 'in the order of their dates' and so overseeing the production of a continuous archive in which nothing is absent. Roger Chartier has described the *Éloge* as a manifesto for a new kind of encounter with books that 'abolishes every distinction between the world of the text and the world of the reader'.[2] But it is significant that at this point the aspect of 'the world of the text' that Diderot most throws himself into is not one of sexual intrigues and contentions over estates, but instead the more mundane and harmless drudgery of editing collections of letters. While Richardson's didactic project is dependent on his readers imagining themselves undertaking similar dilemmas to those of his protagonists, the character Diderot seems to propose to identify with most is the editorial persona adopted by Richardson himself.

This chapter examines the final stretch of the novel after Clarissa has escaped from Lovelace and is awaiting her death. As I have been proposing throughout this book, the tragic trajectory of the novel is that the received notions that Richardson shows to be underpinning the smooth running of the world of the dominant parties, the Harlowes and the rakes, meet a limit in Clarissa's excessive refusal to comply with them any longer after the caesural event of the rape. We saw in the previous two chapters how that event is marked, first, by the introduction of a new and violently disruptive form of quotation in Clarissa's discourse and, second, by an excess of mediation and inhibition in Lovelace's. What is left is to consider how the novel looks at the world after this intervention of tragedy. The two impulses that the real death of Richardson momentarily inspired in Diderot – one of demolishing meaning in the pile of letters and another of propping it up via the editorial process of reordering them – are revealing because they are already part of what Richardson imbues the final phase of his novel with. As I will attempt to show here, the final instalment of *Clarissa* is organised around one impulse to break the novel's meaning up into allegorical mysteries and undecipherable enigmas and another that involves recovering narrative order through exaggerated editorial interventions. Both of these tendencies and the dialectical relationship they come to form are also familiar from Walter Benjamin's account of the German *Trauerspiel* in the seventeenth century. As discussed in my introduction, for Benjamin, the writing of the baroque era was characterised by the crumbling of every principle and institution to so many allegorical 'dry rebuses': desacralised, enigmatic and creaturely. But at the same time, and in keeping with Benjamin's maxim 'the Renaissance explores the universe; the baroque explores libraries', the period's artworks also exhibited another apparently contrary tendency towards taxonomy, editorial organisation and scholarly reference.[3]

Several readers have seen *Clarissa*'s 'dramatic contrasts, its attempts to relate a lower to a higher world, its portrayal of a saintly martyr, its religious ecstasy, and its obsession with the elegiac and funerary' as being in keeping with an ongoing strain of 'baroque style' in the English eighteenth century.[4] Its characteristic register of tomb sculpture, emblematic coffin engravings, dream interpretation, equivocating coded letters and apotheosis paintings seem to cast the novel's final volumes in particular as a recollection of the enigmatic, allegorical side of the baroque as Benjamin describes it. On the other hand, Richardson's habit of raiding anthologies and recycling his own works into new ones, his moments of weirdly detailed specificity about *which* fictional letters are supposed to have gone into his novels and his habit of adding explanatory notes and meaningful alterations in successive editions all align his work with the obsessively 'academic' tendency within the baroque that Benjamin writes of.[5] Indeed, critics have sometimes framed Richardson's editorial interventions as precisely a reaction to the chaotic interpretive openness the first of these tendencies inevitably gives rise to, and, in particular, have seen the alterations and editorial footnotes made and added in the third edition of *Clarissa* as a belated attempt to skew his monstrously ambiguous text in favour of a single definable interpretation and account of its narrative.[6]

In considering the relationship between these two tendencies in *Clarissa*'s final instalment, I begin by showing that even before Richardson made the revisions he did to the third edition of *Clarissa*, there was already a baroque strain in the final instalment pulling the novel towards a self-defeatingly convoluted ideal of scholarly order. I argue that this takes the principal form of the temptation Richardson refers to of giving the novel a 'narrative turn' (C 36) – a single summarisable account to replace the otherwise competing representations of the epistolary novel – and that such a tendency hovers over Lovelace and Belford's representations of Clarissa as well as the interventions of the editorial Richardson at this point in the text.

I

In the preface as it appears in *Clarissa*'s first edition, Richardson says that the novel he purports to be editing is to be based 'principally' on 'a double yet separate correspondence' (C 35). The exchange between Clarissa and Anna and that between Lovelace and Belford are to run parallel, and, while they often comment on the same events, their separation means that no finally unified relationship between their respective interpretations can be insisted on. But at the same time, the preface also acknowledges an alternative organisational model that the book could have taken:

> One gentleman ... of whose knowledge, judgement, and experience, as well as candour, the editor has the highest opinion advised him to give a narrative turn to the letters, and to publish only what concerned the principal heroine – striking off the collateral incidents and all that related to the second characters; ... being extremely fond of the affecting story, he was desirous to have everything parted with, which he thought retarded its progress.

> This advice was not relished by other gentlemen. They insisted that the story could not be reduced to a dramatic unity, nor thrown into the narrative way, without divesting it of its warmth and of a great part of its efficacy. (C 35–6)

Adopting his habitual pose of the great collaborator, Richardson sets his gentlemen advisers against each other, one side coming out for epistolary completeness, the other for stripping things down to the core story. Richardson was notoriously more interested in being seen to seek advice than he was in actually taking it, and the important thing about the passage is neither the phoney debate nor Richardson's other claim here that rather than choosing firmly between the two modes he intends to 'present the world the two first volumes by way of specimen' and play it by ear after that.[7] More significant is how clearly the passage shows the extent to which Richardson was prepared to frame epistolary writing as fundamentally different to any kind of more ordered and continuous narrative. The reliable watchwords of classical storytelling 'dramatic unity' and 'progress' are the preserve of the latter, but complying with them, Richardson suggests, would mean 'reduc[ing]' and 'divesting' the project of what is most valuable about it. The 'narrative way' is not something to aspire to but rather something one might be 'thrown into', as if by mistake.

Richardson's commitment to the model of a 'double yet separate correspondence' against any kind of 'narrative turn' subsequently becomes clear enough. Yet readers have often picked up on moments where his texts seem to be momentarily 'thrown into the narrative way' all the same, suspending their epistolarity in favour of something more like a single-voiced continuous narrative. Ian Watt writes of how in *Pamela*, 'the epistolary convention itself gradually broke down, the letters turned into "Pamela's Journal", and the later parts of the novel therefore produced a kind of narrative effect not unlike that of the autobiographical memoir of Defoe'.[8] Patricia Meyer Spacks comments on the long sequence in *Sir Charles Grandison* in which Harriet relates to Lucy the narrative of the life and death of Sir Charles's father, Sir Thomas (SCG I, 310–86): an account 'gather'd' by Harriet during her time with the Grandison daughters, 'from what was dropt by one lady, and by the other, at different times' (SCG I, 311). Spacks describes this as a sequence in which 'Richardson's famous technique of "writing to the moment" has oddly changed', and 'Harriet writes not to the moment of her own experience, but to that of someone else's narration of long-past experience'.[9] For Leah Price, Richardson's decision in *Clarissa*'s postscript to quickly paraphrase rather than reprint any of the letters he refers to receiving from his female readers offering their own suggestions for plot developments constitutes an 'eleventh-hour repudiation of the epistolary mode' in favour of a single-voiced editor who finally comes out as unwilling to countenance versions of the novel's events other than his own.[10] And Margaret Anne Doody's discussion of the French valet De la Tour's translated account of Lovelace's death in the novel's final letter also frames it as part of such a belated 'repudiation', replacing any account written 'while the hearts of the writers must be supposed to be wholly engaged in their subjects' (C 35), with a 'brief description, in which the narrative viewpoint is … that of a detached observer'.[11]

These examples suggest that whatever Richardson's commitment to epistolary communication, an alternative 'narrative way' also hangs over his works as a dangerous possibility or even temptation, and that this tendency seems to be exacerbated in *Clarissa*'s later parts. If – as I think it is – this is a tendency that marks the final instalment as a whole, it may be that it is actually somehow structural to it, and imposed at the level of the plot. The first two-thirds of the novel are characterised by fierce debate between the correspondents in anticipation of the looming catastrophe, and, during the time that Lovelace and Clarissa are lodged together, by competing accounts in their respective letters of what are often the same, shared experiences. After the rape and Clarissa's subsequent escape however, the novel is increasingly dominated by Belford's accounts of Clarissa's activities and Lovelace's reflections on them, while simultaneously showing characters gradually informing each other of the foregoing events that could not be narrated at the time.

We can see this tendency at work in Letter 349, which documents one of Belford's early visits to Clarissa at the Covent Garden home of Mr and Mrs Smith, the humble shopkeeper couple with whom she lodges until her death. Speaking of the humiliating arrest she has recently suffered on charges of debt invented by the libertine Mrs Sinclair, Clarissa reiterates in characteristically Antigone-like terms the unshakeableness of her position even in the face of such adversity:

> Those who arrested and confined me, no doubt thought they had fallen upon the ready method to distress me so as to bring me into all their measures. But I presume to hope that I have a mind that cannot be debased, in *essential instances*, by *temporary calamities*: little do those poor wretches know of the force of innate principles. (C 1103)

Whatever shifting and contingent disasters occur around her from now on, Clarissa's commitment is such that she will simply continue through them, and this is the surprising truth her antagonists cannot comprehend. This colours her response to Belford, when, slightly earlier in the meeting, he raises once again the question of her forgiving Lovelace and permitting him to make amends: 'you may let him know ... that I reject him with my whole heart – yet that, although I say this with such a determination as shall leave no room for doubt, however I say it not with passion' (C 1101). There is nothing so merely personal as resentment or anger in this rejection any longer. Like Antigone's commitment to the strange other within constituted by the drive in Lacan's interpretation, or like the biblical Job from whom she quotes so often at this stage, such human-all-too-human blandishments are dropping away from her.[12] There is a sad and quite subtle recognition of this when Mrs Smith invites Belford and Clarissa to dine with the couple since it is their wedding anniversary and Clarissa sighs and shakes her head, wishing the pair 'many happy wedding-days' (C 1104) but excusing herself. Clarissa, we might say, admires plenty of things about the world still, but in the commitment she has made they are no longer for her.

The letter, then, captures much of what I have been describing as the tragic in *Clarissa*, most especially the heroine's refusal to comply any longer or to allow amends to be made and normality returned to. But if we have seen that the novel often registers this collapsing of received notions with mad or enigmatic utterances and stultifying breakdowns of communication, in this instance it also supplies an opportunity for the rejected 'narrative turn' to momentarily kick in. Clarissa takes this moment to give what she calls 'a little history of myself', extending over several pages and notably adopting the very language of novel's subtitle: 'The History of a Young Lady'. Like Harriet taking the role of editorial 'gatherer' to the Grandison family history, these early indicators of Clarissa's increasing otherworldliness are accompanied by her slipping into the baroque habit of attempting to add a complete and objective account of all that has gone before to the already overloaded mess of text.

II

As strange as *Clarissa* is going to become after the rape, its strangeness incorporates another impulse towards bringing things back into order and the glimpses of the 'narrative way' Richardson had supposedly rejected in favour of the epistolary mode that haunt the final instalment are part of this tendency. But these impulses are related to each other dialectically, which we can better see if we turn to Letter 271, written by Lovelace a few days after the rape. Here Lovelace narrates and proceeds to interpret a dream weird enough to be in keeping with the explosion of baroque forms in the novel's final stretch. In the dream, an unknown dowager stops in her coach near the house in which Lovelace is still holding Clarissa captive and proceeds to have Clarissa escape with her with the help of the servant Dorcas. The dowager takes Clarissa to a house 'not far from Lincoln's Inn Fields … replete with damsels who wrought curiously in muslins, cambricks, and fine linen, and in every good work that industrious damsels love to be employed about, except the loom and the spinning wheel' (C 921). The dowager is then transformed into a bawd, apparently a friend of Mrs Sinclair named 'Mother H', who deceives Clarissa into allowing her to share her bed. In another transformation, Mother H becomes Lovelace, but then – 'quick as thought', Lovelace says, '(for dreams, thou knowest, confine not themselves to the rules of drama)' – the dream races to imagine a whole married life between him, Clarissa and Anna, with the resultant children of the two mothers intermarrying incestuously 'to consolidate their mammas' friendships'.

Gerald Henry Levin notes that the detail where Lovelace substitutes himself for Clarissa's female sleeping companion retreads his earlier attempt to compel Clarissa to share her bed with the disguised prostitute Miss Partington (see C 538–9).[13] It may even be more similar to the scene in *Pamela* where what seems to be the drunk servant Nan sleeping in Pamela's room reveals itself to be the disguised Mr B (P 199), as if Richardson were allowing Lovelace to dream of his own earlier novel. Lovelace says that dreams do not submit 'to the rules of drama', recalling Richardson's remark that epistolary novels cannot be 'reduced to a dramatic unity'. But of course Lovelace only says as much in the very act of turning his dream's motley accumulation of scenes and images 'into a narrative', as Terry Castle points out, so that 'it reads like a story, a literary plot in little'.[14] This dream so supposedly hostile to the rules of drama also submits to providing a 'plot' in two further ways, in that it becomes the inspiration for Lovelace's next 'plot' against Clarissa – having Dorcas pretend to collaborate in an escape after which Lovelace will rape Clarissa again – which once attempted of course becomes part of the 'plot' of the novel itself.

Richardson's turning enigmatic dreams into points of plot would become the object of scrutiny a few years later. In an anonymous pamphlet entitled *A Candid Examination of the History of Sir Charles Grandison* (1754), published immediately after the appearance of that novel's final instalment,

Francis Plumer comments on the 'extraordinary dream of Miss *Byron*'s, in the sixth volume', saying that Richardson 'has worked it up with a studied confusion and incoherence, to appear the more like dreams, when the mind is disturbed in sleep'.[15] Whereas Lovelace's dream has some albeit unpredictable narrative progression, Harriet's dream is more like a series of isolated takes on the same repeated scene: the possibility of marriage between her and Sir Charles. In one vision he rejects her, in another they are married but he is in love with Clementina, while in others, echoing Lovelace's idea of fathering children by Clarissa and Anna, Harriet sees herself holding Sir Charles's baby by her friend Lucy Selby, and then one by his ward, Emily Jervois. Finally, Harriet dreams that her own earlier suitor, John Greville, has murdered Sir Charles (SCG III, 148–9). If Harriet's dream lacks Lovelace's narrative consistency, it nonetheless shares its odd way of intervening into the novel's 'plot' as it develops subsequently: a few letters later, Greville does indeed threaten to murder Sir Charles (SCG III, 177).

In Plumer's view, Richardson is flirting with the vulgar belief in the clairvoyant properties of dreams held by 'fanciful people', who 'when any thing happens that has a similitude to circumstances that appeared in a dream ... say their dream is out', and so risks compromising his own claims to verisimilitude: 'Mr *R—n's* opinion in regard to dreams, may seem to be a little doubtful'.[16] But the question had already been explicitly addressed in *Clarissa*. For as long as Clarissa seems to be complying with his scheme to have her attempt to escape with Dorcas, Lovelace indeed believes that his 'dream is out' in this way. 'I shall always have a prodigious regard to dreams henceforward', he half-jokes to Belford, 'I know not but I may write a book upon that subject' – '*Lovelace's Reveries*' – 'for my own experiences will furnish out a great part of it' (C 924). When Clarissa incredulously refuses to make the escape with Dorcas however, Lovelace immediately becomes an aggressive Plumer-like sceptic about dreams, dismissing them as 'illusions of fancy depraved, and run mad' (C 927). Castle goes as far as to settle on this as the turning point where Lovelace's assumption to anticipate Clarissa's behaviour begins to break down, as 'the plot fails because Clarissa acts in a way not "predicted" by the dream'. At the same time, Castle notes, tangential similarities between Clarissa's later actual escape and Lovelace's dream mean that the dream somehow *does* go on to influence the plot all the same.[17]

Lovelace and Harriet's dreams, then, are in themselves positioned to oscillate between the baroque tendencies of breaking and remaking meaning, taking chances with verisimilitude while coding plot points in advance. What happens in *Clarissa* next though provides yet another twist of this kind: entangling the disruptive allegorical dream still further in the apparently opposite 'ordering' tendency of the Richardsonian 'narrative turn'. As Lovelace begins to explain his loss of faith in the clairvoyant power of dreams by narrating Clarissa's last-minute refusal, he is abruptly cut off by an unprecedented intervention from Richardson in his editorial persona: 'Mr Lovelace gives here a very circumstantial relation of all that passed between the lady and Dorcas. But as he could only guess at her motives for refusing to go off … it is thought proper to omit his relation' (C 926). This 'editorial' Richardson offers a number of reasons for omitting or abridging letters at other points in the novel. The most benign one is that the letters in question would substantially repeat material appearing in those of others (see for instance, C 524 and 704). A different excuse comes up in Lovelace's fantasy about raping Anna and her mother, omitted in the first edition for the psychologically ham-fisted reason that it doesn't matter because Lovelace '*does not intend to carry it into execution*' (C 671).[18] The explanation for the editorial intervention into Lovelace's account of his dream's predictions, however, is different. Never before has a character's voice been deprived of a place in the novel's archive merely for getting things wrong. Lovelace may well be ill placed to understand Clarissa's reasons for holding back from complying with his fake escape plan. But unfounded 'circumstantial' speculations are the meat and bones of the epistolary form, so it can only strike us as odd that they should become grounds for exclusion now.

In place of whatever it was Lovelace had to say, an editorial summary from Richardson suddenly uncovers 'some *memoranda* of the lady's' (C 926), a book in which we are belatedly told she has been making 'minutes of everything' since the rape 'in order to help her memory – which ... she could less trust to since her late disorders'. While the double yet separate correspondence of epistolary communication has pulsed on, Richardson has concealed underneath it all a single-voiced authoritative account ready for him – or Clarissa – to refer to should the disorder get too great.[19] The significance of this will be underlined when a memorandum book turns up once more after Clarissa's death. Clarissa's will is prefaced with a 'preamble' in which she tries to close down any questions as to whether she was 'of a *sound mind* and *memory*' when she wrote it:

> I for some time past employed myself in penning down heads of such a disposition; which as reasons offered, I have altered and added to; so that I never was absolutely destitute of a *will*, had I been taken off ever so suddenly. These minutes and imperfect sketches enabled me, as God has graciously given me time and sedateness, to digest them into the form in which they appear. (C 1412)

Clarissa's will has not been left to the moment when death is actually at hand but has instead been a continuous process of minute-taking, looking forward to a final act of archiving and anthology-making when the final will actually gets written down. As the editorial Richardson momentarily resorts to the memorandum book to block out Lovelace, Clarissa uses it here to block out possible questions about the stability of her agency and her authority to act as the document's signatory.

It would be in keeping with Richardson's general scrupulousness and specificity about the quiet destinies of the writing materials in his novels if we were to take it that these two books with such similar functions were intended to be the same. Were we tempted to wonder how Clarissa got hold of a memorandum book while at Mrs Sinclair's, Richardson has already made it clear that there is at least one knocking about the place. Coaching Dorcas to request writing lessons from Clarissa early in her captivity there, Lovelace says he '*has given her* [Dorcas] *an ivory-leaved pocketbook with a silver pencil, that she may make memoranda on occasion*' (C 570). This kind of memorandum or 'table' book with erasable ivory pages had been available since the sixteenth century and continued to be popular into the nineteenth.[20] They have also had a small history as a metaphor, from Hamlet saying 'from all the table of my memory / I'll wipe away all trivial fond records' (I.v.98–9) to indicate how his new commitment to avenging his father has erased all prior ones, to Jonathan Swift's 'Verses Wrote in a Lady's Ivory Table-Book', which plays on the temporary status of anything written inside it to make it the ideal medium for recording vacuous or fickle feelings.[21] Later, the table-book also provides a habitual conceit in Anna Letitia Barbauld's poetry as a metaphor for the mind, indeed, in ways that look forward to the appropriations of the twentieth-century equivalent – the 'mystic writing pad' – by Freud and Derrida.[22] Part of what makes such books with erasable pages such a productive conceit for these last two authors is that while these technologies conveniently allow their users to wipe away old notes when they become unwanted, they also tend to leave a perceivable scratched-in trace of everything that has been written on them before. Perhaps this hangs over the hint that, at these key moments, Clarissa is using one. Richardson poses memorandum books against Lovelace's account of his dream and its consequences as two conflicting alternatives to the usual running of the epistolary novel. Later, he will use the memorandum book once again to prop up Clarissa's will as yet another text whose authority is not supposed to be subject to the continual questioning and ambiguity of a double yet separate correspondence. But the unquestionable missives that are supposed to be recorded on it in order to impose narrative order, are threatened by the simultaneous possibilities that they will simply be wiped clean, or haunted by all the previous messages that have been written there before.

III

From the point of view of Clarissa's actions, the final instalment is preoccupied with two moral conundrums. The first is that Clarissa cannot remain alive and yet cannot be seen to have killed herself. As Jonathan Kramnick has suggested, the long-standing Christian prohibition against suicide 'took on a new urgency around the time of *Clarissa*', in part in response to an increasing visibility of materialist philosophy.[23] At a time when the Italian philosopher Alberto Radicati could be deported for extrapolating the permissibility of suicide from the fact of the mere materiality of the human body, or David Hume have his essay 'On Suicide' refused publication, Richardson had to be cautious to stress that however willingly Clarissa goes towards her death, her willingness is not itself the cause of it. The second is a more subtle one: that Richardson is opposed to allowing that Clarissa be perceived to have lied to Lovelace, and yet, it is integral to the model death she is planning that she manages one way or another to keep him away from her. In both cases, the answer Richardson uncovers involves what Benjamin represents as the flipside of the impulse towards scholarly ordering I have just described: the radical breaking apart of signifier and signified that is found in allegory.

For Benjamin, modernity had been impatient of allegory, which he tends to take in its broadest sense to mean all kinds of emblematic and figural representation. Discussing the critical hostility to the old form of allegory among the German Romantics, Benjamin remarks that for these commentators, 'allegory has not simply lost its meaning by "becoming antiquated". What takes place here ... is a conflict between the earlier and the later form which was all the more inclined to silent settlement in that it was non-conceptual, profound and bitter'.[24] If allegory was treated at best with invidious silence by the German Romantics, then what of the standing of allegory in Richardson's day? The moral fables that litter the eighteenth century's periodical literature, the fanciful pseudonyms adopted in its satires and private exchanges of letters, the habit of personification in its poetry and the Rococo overloading of emblems on its furniture, ornaments and in its printed books: all these suggest ways in which allegory and allegorical thinking remained habitual to eighteenth-century representation. Indeed, *Clarissa*'s own frequent allusions to the Book of Job appeared amid a flurry of debate in response to the argument that Job was to be read only as an allegory for Christ made by William Warburton, himself the author of one of the novel's prefaces.[25]

Trying to put a finger on how this situation differs from the earlier baroque discussed by Benjamin, the experience of walking through a space like the Wallace Collection in London today makes it tempting to see in the eighteenth century a kind of depthless postmodernism to the baroque's saturnine modernism, at least as far as the allegorical adornments of its high-end furnishings, jewellery, miniatures and paintings are concerned. Whereas for Benjamin, the earlier seventeenth century's use of allegory is cut through with mourning for its own fragmentariness, the ostensibly irrelevant classical adornings on these clocks, bookshelves and snuff boxes suggest that certain reaches of eighteenth-century life went on with a backdrop of iconographical images without anyone necessarily having the slightest curiosity about what they might once have meant. William Hogarth's *Tail Piece; or, The Bathos or Manner of Sinking in Sublime Paintings* (1764) makes a similar diagnosis. Showing Father Time collapsed among graves, a hanged corpse and various shattered objects of creative achievement including Hogarth's own concept of the 'line of beauty', the engraving has been interpreted by Ronald Paulson as Hogarth's statement of 'the end of all coherent values'. Paulson compares it to the Hyde Park statuary yard depicted in the first plate in Hogarth's book *The Analysis of Beauty* (1753), in which lead cast copies of the great monuments of classical statuary are scattered about, ready to provide decoration for country gentlemen's gardens. 'Hogarth is asserting that the canonical sculptures were now essentially empty signs', Paulson argues, 'these statues derive from a conventional code (aesthetic and iconographic) with no counterpart in the objective world'.[26] But this articulation is already more or less that made by the image from which Hogarth took inspiration for the *Tail Piece*.[27] Albrecht Dürer's *Melencolia 1* (1514) is framed by Benjamin as the privileged text of an incipient baroque while also serving as what Barbara Hassen has called the 'hidden core' of Benjamin's own work.[28] The engraving depicts a mournful angel, around whom 'the utensils of active life are lying around unused on the floor, as objects of contemplation'.[29]

As Jane O. Newman and Sigrid Weigel have emphasised, Benjamin is responding to an early twentieth-century trend for interpreting Dürer's work as a manifestation of a peculiarly German early modern melancholy, for which 'the traditional symbols of classical and medieval astrological knowledge were in flux', causing 'Melancholy to lay aside the tools of any activity at all, such as those visible at her feet'.[30] Benjamin's innovation is to virtually make a methodology of this, allowing Dürer's image to dominate the figurative language he adopts for talking about other texts and historical currents in the period, as well as his own avowedly fragmentary approach to writing itself. 'Those who looked deeper saw the scene of their existence as a rubbish heap of partial, inauthentic actions', Benjamin argues, because 'in the field of allegorical intuition the image is a fragment, a rune … the dry rebuses which remain contain an insight which is still available to the confused investigator'. Through the lens of Benjamin, Hogarth's *Tail Piece* can be understood in line with *Melencolia 1* as an allegory for a certain kind of allegorical reading itself. As Benjamin has it, because in an allegory 'any person, any object, any relationship can mean absolutely anything else', the 'allegorical intuition' is always to see things stripped of their manifest meanings and piled up as so much interpretive flotsam and jetsam, nonetheless containing an enigmatic insight at last.[31] Hogarth, it seems, had this capacity, and it is in keeping with the tragic strain that overcomes *Clarissa* as it moves from the manifest meanings of repeated received notions to the weirder and more broken forms of writing after the rape.

We will see in a moment that Benjamin's characteristic way of talking about allegory as piled up textual rubble also tends to surround Clarissa at the point of her death. But first we should consider how allegory is also a constituent component of how Clarissa orchestrates that death. In the first edition, Volume VI ends with Lovelace's undignified invasion of the Smiths' shop, attempting to visit Clarissa. In Clarissa's absence, he is handed one of the 'Meditations' she has been compiling while living there, a series of tinkered-with quotations from the Book of Psalms, entitled 'On being hunted by the enemy of my soul' (C 1221). Stumbling through the text, Lovelace takes the point that he is that enemy and that Clarissa is finding an idiom for communicating the wrongs he has done her in the language of the Psalms. On reaching a reference to Clarissa being 'as a sparrow alone upon the house-top' (derived from *Psalms* 102:7), however, Lovelace lights up, making the cack-handed inference that this is a coded message that Clarissa is currently hidden in the Smiths' attic.

This comical instance of Lovelace's unsteadiness with reading allegory is met by an altogether serious one as we cross into Volume VII. The volume opens in an atmosphere of dying badly, as Belford tries to comfort his and Lovelace's friend Belton in his unprepared death. Following this, a letter from Clarissa to Lovelace, written a day after Lovelace's invasion of the Smiths', appears in the novel:

> I HAVE good news to tell you. I am setting out with all diligence for my father's house. I am bid to hope that he will receive his poor penitent with a goodness peculiar to himself [...] So, pray, sir, don't disturb or interrupt me – I beseech you don't – You may in time, possibly, see me at my father's, at least, if it be not your own fault. (C 1233)

Clarissa has no intention of returning to Harlowe Place and certainly no intention of seeing Lovelace there, but the letter, we gradually realise, is supposed to be read allegorically. 'Read but for my *father's house, Heaven*' (C 1274), she will later explain to Belford, revealing the letter to be a veiled admission of her impending death as well as exhortation for Lovelace's own repentance. Benjamin associates such separations of manifest content and intended meaning in allegory with death, and Richardson allows for the same inference in the way that the immediate reception of this allegorical letter is interlaced with reports and reflections on the death of Belton. Belford, indeed, specifies that he comes to read the confusing letter in a state of exhaustion, having seen Belton die only hours earlier and with the corpse still there in the room: 'want of rest, and the sad scene I have before my eyes, have rendered me altogether incapable of accounting for it in any shape' (C 1243).

Lovelace agrees to comply with the letter's request and to leave Clarissa alone, but he becomes increasingly agitated at how little it chimes with the information he is gathering about the Harlowes themselves. Arguing that a man who promises to deliver money to a highwayman in exchange for his life is obligated to keep his word, or else to make a poor valuation on his life, Lovelace considers that whereas his own deceptions are in keeping with his character and as much as anyone expects, 'in this lady ... it would be unpardonable to tell a wilful untruth' (C 1270). This is reiterated in his meeting with Clarissa's cousin, Colonel Morden, just afterwards, in which Lovelace remarks that 'I never knew her once dispense with her word; for she always made it a maxim, that *it was not lawful to do evil that good might come of it*' (C 1288), a sentiment with which Morden agrees. Given the circumstances, this might seem over-precious – or, in Lovelace's case, a bit rich – and it is tempting to agree with Belford's initial appraisal and to 'account for it as an *innocent* artifice' (C 1274). But Clarissa is herself in perfect agreement with such objections to her lying, and the text sets a certain amount of store in emphasising that what she has said is not an outright lie. 'Calamity is the test of integrity', Belford reports Clarissa saying on receiving Lovelace's vow to comply with her wishes, 'I hope I have not taken an inexcusable step' (C 1247).

What allows Clarissa to keep Lovelace away, while getting her off the hook over having lied in doing so, is her claim that 'a *religious* meaning is couched under' (C 1274) the letter's manifest statement: the effect of the letter may be deliberately mendacious, but, as far as the literal words on the page are concerned, it is beyond reproach. In this respect, Lovelace's comparison of 'Gulliver in his abominable Yahoo story ... saying the *thing that is not*' (C 1271) is interestingly inappropriate. Swift's famous phrase for lying, adopted by the perfectly reasoning Houyhnhnms who have never heard of such a thing, is technically the opposite of what Clarissa has done.[32] The thing she has said precisely *is*, but not in the sense that she could assume it would be taken. A more helpful analogue appears earlier in the novel. When Lovelace begins his advances towards marriage with Clarissa after the rape, Belford charges him with wriggling out of quite making his intentions explicit: 'thou writest that in thy *present mood* thou thinkest of marrying; and yet canst so *easily* change thy *mood*' (C 958). He refers to Lovelace's remarks as 'Jesuitical qualifyings' and demands that he clarify that he 'meanest to do honourably by her, in *her own* sense of the word'. 'Jesuitical qualifyings' evokes the doctrine of equivocation, which became well known in English discourse during the trial of the Jesuit priest Henry Garnett for his involvement in the Gunpowder Plot in 1605. Garnett's *The Treatise of Equivocation* (c. 1595) had circulated among the conspirators and counselled that while God abhors lies under any circumstances, he permits equivocation: the use of deliberately ambiguous statements, or even silently adding in one's mind information crucial to making the spoken statement true. According to Garnett, a Jesuit could reply negatively to the question 'Did you attend Mass last week?', as long as he then added in his mind, 'at least not in St. Paul's'.[33]

Richardson's interest in equivocation goes back to *Pamela* and the episode where Pamela tells Mr B that she can't have compromised him by spreading the story of his amorous attempt on her in the summerhouse, because she has 'nobody to talk to, hardly!' (P 27). Seizing on this 'hardly', and knowing that she has certainly told Mrs Jervis for one, B calls Pamela a 'little Equivocator': Pamela may be right in saying that she does not have many interlocutors, but that has not stopped her telling every one of them.[34] While Clarissa is represented as being just as committed to telling the truth as everyone around her seems to assume she should be, Pamela's honesty is, if anything, of even more structural importance in the earlier novel. As the scandalous side-correspondence between Pamela and her mother concocted in Henry Fielding's *Shamela* (1741) so brilliantly shows, Richardson's *Pamela* only works if the letters he provides from Pamela addressed to both her parents are assumed to be consistently honest. With nothing comparable to *Clarissa*'s cacophony of competing forms of documentary evidence to go by, any incidental suggestion that Pamela is capable of dissembling constitutes a grave threat to the novel's entire didactic infrastructure.

Pamela and Clarissa skirt dangerously close to a peculiarly formalistic kind of truth-telling that takes no account of context or audience, or, worse, does take account of these things and deliberately manipulates them. In both cases, what mitigation Richardson offers is made in part with reference to by then curiously unfashionable and historically 'other' early modern forms. If a certain untimeliness hangs over Clarissa's equivocating letter to Lovelace designed to keep him away from her while she is dying, then the same is true of the novel's other great allegorical moment: the scene of Clarissa's death itself. The letter is not the only time Clarissa attaches an allegorical meaning to the word 'house' at this point. While Belford is still puzzling through the letter's meaning, Clarissa turns knowingly to Mrs Lovick, her confidante while at the Smiths', and announces a still-more-bewildering intention to purchase a house of her own. 'I have a man, not a woman, for my executor: and think you that I will leave to his care anything that concerns my own person? – Now Mrs Lovick, smiling, do you comprehend me?' (C 1250). This 'house' (subsequently '*palace*' [C 1306]) turns out to be Clarissa's coffin, which she appals everyone by keeping in her room with her as she waits to die. Clarissa has been careful to announce the belief that to '*purposely* ... run into the arms of death' (C 1117) by neglecting her health would make her as culpable as if she had actively committed suicide after the rape. And yet, as Kramnick has stressed, try as critics may to identify the physiological cause of Clarissa's death, Richardson seems to hold back from committing to any causation whatsoever.[35] She wants to die, and does, but on there being any connection between the two things, or any reason for the second taking place at all, the novel simply stays silent.[36]

The cause of death remains an enigmatic void, but so too does the coffin. Decorated with emblematic 'devices' (C 1305) – a winged hourglass, an urn, a crowned serpent devouring its own tail – and inscribed with quotations from the Book of Psalms and from Job, the coffin tempts us, Castle says, 'to translate or paraphrase it'.[37] But as identifiable as these emblems may be from seventeenth-century emblem books, their meanings do not stay still in the novel. Rather, the coffin's engravings reach out to confuse and multiply in the minds of those who see them. Having seen the coffin, Belford is 'ill and restless all night', dreaming 'of nothing but of flying hour-glasses, death's heads, spades, mattocks, and eternity; the hint of her devices (as given me by Mrs Smith) running in my head' (C 1305). Mrs Smith might have offered to gloss the engravings to Belford, but that doesn't stop him adding images to the coffin that weren't even there in reality, calling to mind the remark from Richardson's edition of *Aesop's Fables* (1739) that 'an emblem without a key to't ... is but one folly grafted upon another' (EW 103). For Paulson, the coffin places *Clarissa* in the century's subterranean tradition of artworks that frame 'baffling central objects', such as those at the heart of Joseph Wright of Derby's paintings, *An Experiment with an Air Pump* (1768), *An Academy by Lamplight* (1769), *The Blacksmith's Forge*, and *Miravan Breaking Open the Tomb of His Ancestors* (both 1771).[38] Without any dependable 'key' to explain them, the images on the coffin take on a talismanic position in the text analogous to that of the mad papers. Shocking and debilitating to all who come into contact with them, they too are an affront to the regime of the received notions.

IV

This chapter has argued that the broken and mournful landscape of *Clarissa* after the rape shares the ambivalent impulses that Benjamin associates with the tragic drama of the German seventeenth century. On the one hand, this phase of the novel initiates a clampdown on the structural uncertainties of the epistolary form, manifested in the subtle attempts Richardson allows in to bring the interpretively unwieldy text into some kind of consistent narrative order. On the other, this impulse towards order is qualified by a proliferation of enigmatic and distorted allegorical forms: dreams, the equivocating letter, the emblem-inscribed coffin, and the unexplained death. Allowing the image of *Melencolia 1* to overtake his language once more, Benjamin remarks that in the *Trauerspiel*, 'destiny is not only divided among the characters', but 'is equally present among the objects'. What this destiny entails is elaborated in Benjamin's characteristic vocabulary for the emblematic objects in the huge range of plays, paintings and treatises he discusses: they petrify, dry up, die away, the life flows out of them, and they become rebuses.[39] Benjamin offers a way of understanding this in the parable of the funeral pyre at the start of his essay on Goethe's *Elective Affinities*. As the material content of the pyre's burning logs collapses away, the bright flame emerging from them 'preserves an enigma' all the same.[40] The object is destined to decay as it gets further and further away from the context that produced it. And yet that decay allows for a however enigmatic new 'truth content' to flame up, liberated from the constraints of how the object was originally understood. This parable also provides a way of understanding the destiny of the received notions that underlies the tragedy of *Clarissa*. They travel from being figures of speech helping to prop up normality in the novel's early volumes to breaking out into a more violent and exploratory form of quotation in the mad papers to, finally, taking their place as a constellation of obscure puzzles in the series of allegories in the final stretch.

Writing of the caesura Hölderlin framed as the prerequisite for tragedy, Benjamin adds that 'one could not characterise this rhythm more aptly than by asserting that something beyond the poet interrupts the language of the poetry'.[41] The present reading of *Clarissa* as a novel interrupted by tragedy may well be very far from anything Richardson himself could have consciously intended or articulated. But what it does share with the 'poet' is the conviction that Clarissa's various refusals, and finally her death itself, represent a radical and strictly ethical act. In this its position differs from that of several very significant readings of the novel, and that difference warrants some comment before we close. The novel's final emblematic figure is the dead body of Clarissa herself, of whom Anna – looking forward to the collation of Clarissa's letters into something resembling the novel itself at the end – had earlier written, 'your story ... will afford a warning as well as an example' (C 1315). This willingness to die and to replace her living body with what William Warner calls 'a new form in which to embody the subject – the story she will eventually have cast into a book' puts Clarissa in an odd position.[42] A character at the forefront of what is commonly interpreted as an increasingly subjective turn in the novel in the mid eighteenth century, Clarissa ends up aspiring to the status of a pre-novelistic allegorical figure.[43] Exchanging the messy contingency of a living body for a single written version of events in the book she begins to construct in her dying weeks, Clarissa also seeks to exchange the novelistic virtues of psychological richness and realistic manners for a single figural value.

Warner has been the most outspoken critic of this dimension of *Clarissa*, charging Richardson (or more usually Clarissa herself) with promulgating a version of what Nietzsche would call 'the ascetic ideal': employing a righteous pose of being hard done by as an excuse for imposing one's will on others.[44] For Warner, Clarissa is as comfortable as she is with death and her transformation into a kind of allegory only because she is able to use it as a mechanism of revenge against Lovelace and the Harlowes. 'By building a book, and putting her friends and adversaries in her book', Warner contends, 'she tries to assume a Godlike authority and dominion over them'.⁴⁵ To adapt Nietzsche's closing words from *On The Genealogy of Morals*, Warner's Clarissa would rather will nothingness than not will at all, and her own destruction is a small price to pay for the reimposition of her will over those who have wronged her.⁴⁶ The debate doesn't need rehearsing here, but it is fair to say that his forceful identification of the usual poststructuralist bêtes noires – liberal humanism, logocentrism, bourgeois morality – with Clarissa personally, and the uncareful note of admiration he strikes when writing of Lovelace, has left the early Warner open to the charge of misogyny.⁴⁷ And yet more than one significant feminist reading of the novel has criticised the representation of Clarissa's death on similar grounds. For Tassie Gwilliam, 'the reconstitution of the female body as inviolable and immune to the pressures of invasion and definition takes place at the expense of life'.⁴⁸ For Judith Broome, not even Clarissa's corpse is free from such malign sublimations: 'Richardson's own ambivalence toward Clarissa is evident here. Although he allows Clarissa to withdraw from circulation within the patriarchal economy through her death, her dying body, as an aesthetic object, is quickly reabsorbed into that economy'.⁴⁹

In their different ways, each of these critics is at least made uneasy by the terms in which Richardson frames Clarissa's liberation in an immaculate death, whether the problematic part be in her preferring to die rather than to live untidily or unjustified, or in the admiring descriptions her 'lovely skeleton' (C 1231) receives when she is on the way out. Certainly, when Clarissa rationalises that if she 'die not now', she might make the mistake of dying at a later, happier time, 'when my heart had beat high with the desire of life and when the vanity of this earth had taken hold of me' (C 1117), it hardly strikes one as taking the side of life. The philosopher most identified with calling out those weak nihilists who prefer perfectibility and transcendence to the blood-and-guts messiness of actual living is Nietzsche. But on those grounds, I would like to argue that a rehabilitation of what is obviously an ideologically problematic part of the novel might be effected by opposing these Nietzsche-style critiques of the satisfaction Richardson takes in Clarissa's death with a Benjaminian one.

To set this up, we can refer to a dream Lovelace has in anticipation of Clarissa's death:

> I thought I would have clasped her in my arms: when immediately the most angelic form I had ever beheld, vested all in transparent white, descended from the ceiling, which opening, discovered a ceiling above that, stuck round with golden cherubs and glittering seraphs, all exulting: Welcome, welcome, welcome! and, encircling my charmer, ascended with her to the region of seraphims; and instantly, the opening ceiling closing, I lost sight of *her*, and of the *bright form* together, and found wrapped in my arms her azure robe (all stuck thick with stars of embossed silver), which I had caught hold of in hopes of detaining her; but was all that was left me of my beloved Miss Harlowe. (C 1218)

As Alison Conway observes, Clarissa has become for Lovelace 'an ascending Virgin Mary in a baroque painting', and such paintings featuring scenes of apotheosis are a point of reference for both Nietzsche and Benjamin.[50] In *The Birth of Tragedy*, Nietzsche interprets the opposition in Raphael's *Transfiguration* (c. 1520) between the transcendent resurrected Christ in the top section and the immanent fractured disaster of the apostles' attempt to exorcise the boy in the lower section, as an expression of the opposition between the Apollonian and Dionysian: Nietzsche's terms for the two elementary ingredients in tragic art. The lower 'Dionysian' section 'shows us the reflection of the eternal original suffering, of the sole ground of the world'. Above it, 'rising like the scent of ambrosia', is the Apollonian, 'which remains invisible to those who are caught in the first world ... a brilliant hovering in purest bliss and painless contemplation through beaming wide-open eyes'.[51] It is surely with a slight smirk that this section is to be read, since the great Christian painting is discussed without any even critical reference to its intended subject matter, so, as one commentator has it, replacing even at the level of the discussion 'the redemptive promise of Christ with the empty splendour of Apollo'.[52]

In this early book, Nietzsche is more willing to regard the Dionysian and Apollonian parts of tragedy as having a reciprocal necessity than he will be later on. Fearing that he had made the Apollonian sound too much like a Schopenhauer's ordering force of 'representation' – not to mention the embarrassing Hegelian tang of the view of tragedy as a synthesising outcome of two opposed forces – Nietzsche distances himself from this dimension of *The Birth of Tragedy* in an 'Attempt at Self Criticism', added to the book 1886.[53] There, Nietzsche finally shows his colours, saying that – never mind the alternative forms of transcendence he had dabbled with in the figure of Apollo – the stress of the book should simply have been that 'Christianity was from the very beginning essentially and fundamentally the disgust and aversion felt by life towards itself, merely disguised, concealed and masquerading under the belief in an "other" or "better" life'.[54] While the Nietzsche of *The Birth of Tragedy* could affirm the Apollonian claim that 'it is only as an *aesthetic phenomenon* that the existence and the world are eternally *justified*', the later Nietzsche becomes steadily less interested in any such aspiration to justification beyond the Dionysian collisions and sufferings of life at the bottom of the painting.[55] From now on, any division of the transcendent from the immanent such as that in the *Transfiguration* will only be the object of Nietzsche's contempt.

The very residual idealism Nietzsche later felt the need to exorcise from his theory earns a scathing reference to 'the abyss of aestheticism' in Benjamin's *Trauerspiel* book. No more likely than the later Nietzsche to fall into an abyssal dislike of the creaturely world, Benjamin has a very different reading of the apotheosis genre to which Raphael's painting and Lovelace's baroque dream belong:

> In paintings of apotheoses, the foreground is generally treated with exaggerated realism so as to be able to show the remoter, visionary objects more reliably. The attempt to gather all worldly events into this graphic foreground is not undertaken only in order to heighten the tension between immanence and transcendence, but also in order to secure for the latter the

greatest conceivable rigour, exclusiveness and inexorability. It is an unsurpassably spectacular gesture to place even Christ in the realm of the provisional, the everyday, the unreliable.[56]

The reversal of the Nietzschean view is disarmingly simple. The Christian tradition might well have divided reality into a worldly immanence and a heavenly transcendence, and the apotheosis paintings may give a literal representation of the divide, but there is still absolutely nothing in the paintings to force us to give any priority to the transcendent as was no doubt intended. On the contrary, Benjamin asks, if the lower 'worldly' sections of these paintings are merely the objects of their scorn or relegation, then how are we to account for the pronounced 'realism' with which the lower sections are often presented? For another Jewish-German critic writing at the time, Erich Auerbach, the achievement of Dante's *Commedia* was precisely comic: it brought the highest notions of the Christian cosmos down to the level of everyday representation.[57] Similarly for Benjamin, far from aspiring to rise haughtily above the material world, the apotheosis paintings actually threaten to drag the higher transcendent content down to the material's baser everyday level. 'The penchant of the baroque for apotheosis is a counterpart to its own particular way of looking at things', says Benjamin, for which there is absolutely nothing so spiritual that is not capable of undertaking 'the seal of the all-too-earthly'.[58]

The critics who have been wary of the idealised death Richardson prepares for Clarissa have tended to be so on the sound Nietzschean basis that 'the belief in an "other" or "better" life' has too often been a disguise for a 'disgust and aversion felt by life towards itself'. But what happens when we bring Benjamin into the equation? The Benjamin who wrote just before his death of the radical potential of a 'theology, which ... is small and ugly and has to keep out of sight' never placed his priorities anywhere other than in the material world but, equally, never saw a metaphysical or even explicitly religious interest as necessarily compromising to that. In Benjamin's dialectical philosophy, the metaphysical tends to be a bit grubby and shop-spoiled – as Benjamin says the authority figures are in Kafka – while the material is always prone to burst into mystical truth-revealing flames.[59] In Lovelace's account of his apotheosis dream, we take, logically enough, Lovelace's perspective, left holding Clarissa's 'azure robe (all stuck thick with stars of embossed silver)' (C 1218) as Clarissa herself ascends into Heaven. I assume that this moment is articulated in full awareness of its camp silliness, but, at the same time, it is actually fairly representative of how Clarissa's death is figured in the novel. Just as Benjamin argues for a priority of the lower, sublunary parts of the apotheosis paintings, Richardson's attempts to draw our attention upwards always meet with the tripwire of the fact that his novel, perhaps of necessity, is always implicitly on the side of the worldly.

This tendency is reflected in the episode we have already touched on in which Clarissa's coffin is brought into her room. Belford reports that as he was speaking with Clarissa,

> a blush overspread her face, on hearing, as I also did, a sort of lumbering noise upon the stairs, as if a large trunk were bringing up between two people: and looking upon me with an eye of concern, Blunderers! said she, they have brought in something two hours before the time. (C 1304)

The arrival of the coffin is enormously significant, introducing into the text one of its key allegorical artefacts, as well as establishing the extent to which Clarissa, insouciant as she is around this material witness to her own impending death, is withdrawing from all codes of normality. And yet the way it is introduced is insistently bathetic, brought in at the wrong time by two blundering deliverymen and announced by the 'lumbering' noise of them trying to get it up the stairs. The comparison that comes to mind is Laurel and Hardy's famous attempt to deliver a piano in *The Music Box* (1932). The pallbearers' struggle when carrying a coffin is today sometimes admired as a physical analogue to the emotional struggle undertaken by the other mourners at a funeral. But the combination of the sombre dignity of the object and the inconvenience of trying to carry it means that, like a smart bourgeois couple's new piano, a coffin threatens to topple over into comedy when subjected to the indignity of being carried upstairs.

As Clarissa exclaims a little earlier, 'how this body clings! – how it encumbers!' (C 1265). E. Derek Taylor may summarise Richardson's religious plan as an attempt 'to justify Providence by immersing his putatively Christian readership within a tragic quagmire from which only faith in "a future reward" offered escape', but that 'quagmire' seems to be the thing that the novel repeatedly aligns itself with.[60] This chapter began by considering Diderot's fantasy of finding Richardson's novels collapsed and scattered into their bare letters, and perhaps this is a more apt image for the novel than Diderot knew. If Clarissa has ascended, then she has done so by leaving us readers and, crucially, the constituent materials of the novel itself lurking in the world of the sublunary. A final example of the novel's treatment of the coffin may illustrate how comfortable the text seems to be with that situation.

Characteristically keen to anticipate any criticism that might be made of her, Clarissa justifies the amount of money she has spent on the coffin on the basis that 'she did not know but her father would permit it, when furnished, to be carried down to be deposited with her ancestors; and in that case she ought not to discredit them in her *last appearance*' (C 1306). In the third edition, Richardson altered the last phrase to 'her *appearance among them*' (3C VII, 313). This small but curious alteration has the effect of completely changing who it is Clarissa is supposed to be appearing before. The first edition deals with Clarissa's 'last *appearance*' among the living at her funeral, but the third edition places the stress on her ongoing '*appearance among*' the dead relatives in the tomb. While the moral project of *Clarissa* aspires upward, the fascination of characteristic details like this is with moving the point of view yet further downward. For Benjamin, the significant thing about martyrdom is not merely the beatification of the soul but also the body that is left behind. 'Martyrdom thus prepares the body of the living person for emblematic purposes', says Benjamin, 'and the characters of the Trauerspiel die because it is only thus, as corpses, that they can enter into the homeland of allegory'. Clarissa joins these *Trauerspiel* figures in a preparation of her body that pulls as much attention to the material and sublunary as it does to the transcendent. As Benjamin has it, 'it is not for the sake of immortality' that these figures 'meet their end, but for the sake of the corpse'.[61]

Notes

1 Denis Diderot, *Selected Writings on Art and Literature*, ed. and trans. Geoffrey Bremner (Harmondsworth: Penguin, 1994), p. 87; for comment on Richardson's influence on Diderot, see P. N. Furbank, *Diderot: A Critical Biography* (London: Secker & Warburg, 1992), pp. 209–10; and James Fowler, '*La Religieuse*: Diderot's "Richardsonian" Novel', in James Fowler (ed.), *New Essays on Diderot* (Cambridge: Cambridge University Press, 2011), pp. 127–38.
2 Roger Chartier, *Inscription and Erasure: Literature and Written Culture from the Eleventh to the Eighteenth Century*, trans. Arthur Goldhammer (Philadelphia, Pa.: University of Pennsylvania Press, 2005), p. 111.
3 Benjamin, *The Origin of German Tragic Drama*, pp. 176, 140.
4 William Park, '*Clarissa* as Tragedy', *Studies in English Literature*, 16 (3) (1976): 461–71 (p. 470); see also Watt, *The Rise of the Novel*, p. 218: 'to his contemporaries … Richardson's funerary emphasis would have seemed justified for its own sake; and we, perhaps, can only try to regard it in the same light as we do a good deal of baroque memorial sculpture – forget the crushing banality of the symbolism and notice only the elaborate assurance of its presentation'. One pauses over this passage to remember that one of the most scrupulous readers of the Benjamin's *Trauerspiel* book, Theodor Adorno, is thanked in Watt's acknowledgements for his scholarly advice.
5 Benjamin, *The Origin of German Tragic Drama*, p. 160.
6 For the critical development of this view of Richardson's revisions, see Gerard A. Barker, 'Clarissa's "Command of Her Passions": Self-Censorship in the Third Edition', *Studies in English Literature 1500–1900*, 10 (3) (1970): 525–39; Warner, *Reading Clarissa*, pp. 180–218; Castle, *Clarissa's Ciphers*, pp. 175–80; and Keymer, *Richardson's Clarissa*, pp. 246–8.

7 Richardson's friend, Aaron Hill, suggested that the original for the first interlocutor was probably Colley Cibber, although Hill himself had also recommended cutting Clarissa; see Christine Gerrard, *Aaron Hill: The Muses' Projector, 1685–1750* (Oxford: Oxford University Press, 2003), pp. 214–19.
8 Watt, *The Rise of the Novel*, p. 209.
9 Patricia Meyer Spacks, *Boredom: The Literary History of a State of Mind* (Chicago, Ill.: University of Chicago Press, 1995), pp. 130–1.
10 Price, *The Anthology and the Rise of the Novel*, p. 27.
11 Margaret Anne Doody, *A Natural Passion: A Study of the Novels of Samuel Richardson* (Oxford: Clarendon Press, 1974), p. 179.
12 On Richardson's contradictory evocation of Job as a figure of 'the suppression of the particulars of individual suffering', see Jonathan Lamb, *The Rhetoric of Suffering: Reading the Book of Job in the Eighteenth Century* (Oxford: Clarendon Press, 1995), p. 227.
13 Gerald Henry Levin, *Richardson the Novelist: The Psychological Patterns* (Amsterdam: Rodopi, 1978), p. 61.
14 Terry Castle, *The Female Thermometer: 18th Century Culture and the Invention of the Uncanny* (Oxford: Oxford University Press, 1995), p. 59.
15 [Francis Plumer], *A Candid Examination of the History of Sir Charles Grandison* (London, 1754), p. 24.
16 [Plumer], *A Candid Examination*, pp. 25, 27.
17 Castle, *The Female Thermometer*, pp. 60–1.
18 The letter is then included in full in 3C IV, 252–61.
19 In Letter 276, a short while later, the editorial Richardson employs the conceit of the memorandum book once again to correct errors of fact made by Lovelace.
20 For an expansive account, see Peter Stallybrass, Roger Chartier, J. Franklin Mowery and Heather Wolfe, 'Hamlet's Tables and the Technologies of Writing in Renaissance England', *Shakespeare Quarterly*, 55 (4) (2004): 379–419.
21 See Jonathan Swift, 'Verses Wrote in a Lady's Ivory Table-Book' in *The Complete Poems*, ed. Pat Rogers (Harmondsworth: Penguin, 1983), pp. 81–2.
22 See Anna Letitia Barbauld, 'Verses Written in the Leaves of an Ivory Table Book' and 'Love and Time', in *The Poems*, ed. William McCarthy and Elizabeth Kraft (Athens, Ga.: University of Georgia Press, 1994), pp. 27–8, 94–6; and Jacques Derrida,

'Freud and the Scene of Writing', in *Writing and Difference*, trans. Alan Bass (London: Routledge, 2001), pp. 246–91.
23 Kramnick, *Actions and Objects*, pp. 220–3.
24 Benjamin, *The Origin of German Tragic Drama*, p. 161.
25 See Lamb, *The Rhetoric of Suffering*, Chapter 6.
26 Ronald Paulson, *Breaking and Remaking: Aesthetic Practice in England, 1700–1820* (New Brunswick: Rutgers University Press, 1989), p. 212.
27 For comment on Hogarth's intellectual and religious sympathy with Dürer, see Ronald Paulson, *Hogarth's Harlot: Sacred Parody in Enlightenment England* (Baltimore, Md.: The Johns Hopkins University Press, 2003), p. 149.
28 Barbara Hanssen, 'Portrait of Melancholy (Benjamin, Warburg, Panofsky)', *MLN*, 114 (5) (1999): 991–1013 (p. 1000).
29 Benjamin, *The Origin of German Tragic Drama*, p. 140.
30 Sigrid Weigel, *Walter Benjamin: Images, the Creaturely, and the Holy*, trans. Chadwick Truscott Smith (Palo Alto, Calif.: Stanford University Press, 2013), p. 211; Newman, *Benjamin's Library*, p. 163; as Newman shows, this was dominated by, but by no means limited to, the work of Aby Warburg's followers.
31 Benjamin, *The Origin of German Tragic Drama*, pp. 139, 176, 175.
32 See Jonathan Swift, *Gulliver's Travels*, ed. Claude Rawson (Oxford: Oxford University Press, 2005), p. 219.
33 On Garnett, see Frank L. Huntley, '*Macbeth* and the Background of Jesuitical Equivocation', *PMLA*, 79 (4) (1964): 390–400.
34 For more discussion of the episode and the significance of equivocation, see Jenny Davidson, *Hypocrisy and the Politics of Politeness: Manners and Morals from Locke to Austen* (Cambridge: Cambridge University Press, 2004), pp. 123–8.
35 Kramnick, *Actions and Objects*, p. 228; for a survey of suggested causes, none of which, Kramnick argues, are strictly supportable, see pp. 296–8n67.
36 For the remarkable argument that – physiological causes aside – eighteenth-century law might have considered Lovelace guilty of the 'felony murder' of Clarissa, see Macpherson, *Harm's Way*, Chapter 2.
37 Castle, *Clarissa's Ciphers*, p. 142; for one attempt to gloss the emblems, see Doody, *A Natural Passion*, p. 186.
38 Paulson, *Breaking and Remaking*, p. 222.
39 Benjamin, *The Origin of German Tragic Drama*, pp. 132, 166, 176, 182, 183, 176.

40 Benjamin, *Selected Writings*, vol. I, p. 268.
41 Benjamin, *Selected Writings*, vol. I, p. 341.
42 Warner, *Reading Clarissa*, p. 92.
43 For an analysis of the tensions such a view of subjectivity is placed under in *Sir Charles Grandison*, see Rebecca Anne Barr, 'Richardson's *Sir Charles Grandison* and the Symptoms of Subjectivity', *The Eighteenth Century: Theory and Interpretation*, 51 (4) (2010): 1–24.
44 See Nietzsche, *On the Genealogy of Morals*, pp. 96–7.
45 Warner, *Reading Clarissa*, p. 75.
46 Nietzsche, *On the Genealogy of Morals*, p. 136.
47 See Castle, *Clarissa's Ciphers*, pp. 192–6.
48 Tassie Gwilliam, *Samuel Richardson's Fictions of Gender* (Palo Alto, Calif.: Stanford University Press, 1993), p. 105.
49 Judith Broome, *Fictive Domains: Body, Landscape, and Nostalgia, 1717–1770* (Plainsboro, NJ: Associated University Presses, 2010), p. 47.
50 Alison Margaret Conway, *Private Interests: Women, Portraiture, and the Visual Culture of the English Novel: 1709–1791* (Toronto: University of Toronto Press, 2001), p. 104.
51 Nietzsche, *The Birth of Tragedy*, p. 31.
52 James McFarland, *Constellation: Friedrich Nietzsche and Walter Benjamin in the Now-Time of History* (New York: Fordham University Press, 2013), p. 112.
53 The 'Hegelian' charge appears in Nietzsche's second critique of *The Birth of Tragedy* in *Ecce Homo*; see Friedrich Nietzsche, *Ecce Homo*, trans. R. J. Hollingdale (London: Penguin, 2004), p. 48.
54 Nietzsche, *The Birth of Tragedy*, p. 9; on the 'inscrutable silence, not exactly hostile and punctuated by a few, more or less complimentary, characterisations' that marks the treatment of Christianity in the first edition of *The Birth of Tragedy*, see M. S. Silk and J. P. Stern, *Nietzsche on Tragedy* (Cambridge: Cambridge University Press, 1984), p. 114.
55 Nietzsche, *The Birth of Tragedy*, p. 38.
56 Benjamin, *The Origin of German Tragic Drama*, pp. 103, 183.
57 See Erich Auerbach, *Dante: Poet of the Secular World*, trans. Ralph Manheim (New York: New York Review of Books, 2007), p. 134.
58 Benjamin, *The Origin of German Tragic Drama*, p. 180; Benjamin had put this another way in his essay on Socrates. Evoking the

green halo in Matthias Grünewald's *Resurrection of Christ* (part of the *Isenheim Altarpiece*, c. 1515), Benjamin says that 'Grünewald painted the saints with such grandeur that their halos emerged from the greenest black. The radiant is true only where it is refracted in the nocturnal; only there is it expressionless, only there is it asexual and yet of supramundane sexuality' (*Selected Writings*, vol. I, p. 53); see Weigel, *Walter Benjamin*, pp. 219–24.
59 Benjamin, *Selected Writings*, vol. IV, p. 389, vol. II, p. 796.
60 Taylor, *Reason and Religion in Clarissa*, p. 111.
61 Benjamin, *The Origin of German Tragic Drama*, pp. 217–18.

Conclusion

This book began by suggesting that Richardson's claim that he wrote *Clarissa* to challenge his public's faith in a 'dangerous but too commonly received notion' is, first, more surreptitiously significant to the novel as a whole than is usually thought, and, second, structurally related to its tragedy. In Chapter 1, I argued that the novel explores a quite flexible and varied idea of what a 'received notion' might be – whether a rumour, the way family members might back each other up by repeating each other, or the inversely moral maxims used by rakes – and that such self-confirming statements are a constituent part of the persecution of Clarissa that Richardson represents in the novel's early volumes. In Chapters 2 and 3, I showed, from the perspectives of Clarissa and Lovelace respectively, how preoccupied the novel becomes with the limits of such quotational forms of authority, specifically at the caesural juncture of the rape. Finally, in Chapter 4, I drew on Walter Benjamin's vocabulary for describing the baroque to examine the accelerated half-life of the received notions in the novel's final sections: their collapse into various fragmented allegories.

Part of this last argument was that one of the tendencies of the novel's strange and *Trauerspiel*-like last stretch is a perceivable editorial impulse to close down on the opposing epistolary narratives that have hitherto run alongside each other. I want to return to and briefly reassess the significance of this point here, in an 'attempt at self-criticism' of my own. From the Introduction onwards, I have tended to agree with those critics who have suggested in passing that the character from tragedy that Clarissa can most helpfully be compared to is Sophocles' Antigone: in particular as Jacques Lacan represents her in his seminar on *The Ethics of Psychoanalysis*. For Lacan, *Antigone* is the play most commensurate with *the* ethical, theoretical and therapeutic insight of psychoanalysis: that analysis is not there to help you change inconvenient or destructive desires, nor to domesticate your desire into a neatly maintained lifestyle choice, but rather seeks to allow you to take up the mantle of your desire and to find a vocabulary for situating yourself within its break. Clarissa's remarkably resilient work of positioning herself in this way is – I have tried to show from Chapter 2 onwards – represented by Richardson as the direct cause of the breakdown of the received notions that have been permitted to reign in the novel prior to this. It is Clarissa's own refusal to give ground in this way that the novel symptomatises in the caesural break it introduces at the point of the rape itself. And this is what makes the novel consistent with Friedrich Hölderlin's notion that both Benjamin and Lacan invoke:

> the rhythmic succession of ideas wherein the *transport* manifests itself demands a counter-rhythmic interruption, a pure word, *that which in metrics is called a caesura*, in order to confront the speeding alternation of ideas at its climax, so that not the alternation of the idea, but the idea itself appears.[1]

But what if that tendency towards 'counter-rhythmic interruption' actually runs deeper in *Clarissa* than the obvious interruption of the rape and the other interruptions-in-miniature that (in Chapters 2 and 3) I have argued surround it? This is the qualification to the book's whole argument that I want to raise here.

I have been wrestling with Richardson's own analysis of what was distinctive about the epistolary novel as opposed to other kinds of narrative throughout this book, but let us return here to Richardson's remark that *Clarissa* was written 'principally in a double yet separate correspondence: between two young ladies of virtue and honour … and between two gentlemen of free lives'. The passage continues:

the letters on both sides are written while the hearts of the writers must be supposed to be wholly engaged in their subjects: the events at the time generally dubious – so that they abound not only with critical situations, but with what may be called instantaneous descriptions and reflections, which may be brought home to the heart of the youthful reader. (C 36)

What brings the novel's letters 'home to the heart' is precisely how 'dubious' the outcome of the events they detail are at the time of writing. Once again, the epistolary form is one of dialectical contrasts: its vividness the result of obscurity, its fidelity to the instant the result of its missives always lagging slightly behind whatever it is that is going on. Aaron Hill, a commentator whose editorial recommendations have not been remembered admiringly by Richardson scholars, seized on something of this effect when commenting on an early draft of *Clarissa* in 1746. Hill refers to 'a fine effect that rises very often (where you proposed it *should* rise) from different views and principles, of persons to whom the same fact is related: and their different reflections (from contrasted passions) which that one event produces'.[2] Hill, it seems, is not especially interested in the idea that these 'different views' might eventually be reconciled, nor, indeed, as the position sometimes attributed to Richardson has it, is he necessarily interested in seeing in the novel a way of training the reader to know which viewpoint to accept as trustworthy.[3] Instead, this 'fine effect' emerges specifically in the irreconcilable point of difference between the views and reflections 'that one event produces', in what we could go as far as to call an aesthetics of difference.

Discussing 'the invention and refinement' of free indirect discourse in the nineteenth century, Andrew Bennett argues that this 'new narrative technology that above all other drives the development of the post-Romantic novel' worked to clamber above the increasingly diverse and discordant character of modern society, in the hope of replacing the experience of irreducible ignorance that brought, with some sort of reassuring continuity. In Bennett's view, a characteristic achievement of the liberal project of the nineteenth-century novel like

Middlemarch can be understood as 'a vast network of textuality with just one purpose: to comfort the bewildered with a sense ... not only that there are other minds but that we can know them'.[4] If we agree that the tendency of the novel in its 'classic' nineteenth-century incarnation is towards this sense of reconciled and mutual 'knowing', uniting characters and by extension readers, then what if the Richardsonian epistolary novel, by contrast, is *the* form of a certain principled ignorance? Followed to its conclusion, Hill's comment would support such a view: that the articulation of *Clarissa* is that there is something unbridgeable between subjects and, indeed, within their relations to themselves.

Clarissa may reflect to Anna that 'the workings of passion, when indulged, are but too much alike, whether man or woman' (C 641), but we have already seen many instances in which Clarissa and Lovelace seem to be pursuing entirely irreconcilable trajectories, divided by gender as much as genre. As we saw in the Introduction, the rakes favour comedy, in a way that places women on the side of tragedy, and the opposition this implies is suggested by Lovelace's remark that 'the devil's in it, if a confided-in rake does not give a girl enough tragedy in his comedy' (C 618). Susan Staves, discussing the question of why Clarissa does not attempt to legally prosecute Lovelace for the rape, argues that the trial would necessarily be founded on two narratives made irreconcilable by genre: 'the woman's tragic narrative against the man's comic one'.[5] More broadly, the elaborate argument of *Harm's Way: Tragic Responsibility and the Novel Form* (2009) by Sandra Macpherson has identified a tragically anti-humanist and a feminist tendency with Richardson, working against a comic masculinism in Fielding.[6] In the present book, we saw in Chapter 1 that while several of the novel's women are supposed to hold with the received notion that 'reformed rakes make the best husbands', Lovelace and his compatriots maintain that 'once subdued', a woman is 'always subdued', positions which are as irreconcilable as they are perfectly paralleled. Later, as Chapter 3 showed, Lovelace's certainty that Clarissa will forgive and marry him is balanced by Clarissa's equal conviction that she will not. And, finally, as we saw in Chapter 4, Clarissa dies amid her and Lovelace's completely different understanding of the meaning of a single letter.

Richardson's remark that his novel comprises 'a double yet separate correspondence' (C 35), then, should be pushed to take on its strongest possible meaning: that it indicates a commitment at the level of form to a kind of irreducible ignorance or lack of rapport. The great theorist of such states is Lacan. In *The Four Fundamental Concepts of Psychoanalysis*, for instance, Lacan says that 'when, in love, I solicit a look … what is profoundly unsatisfying and always missing is that – *You never look at me from the place from which I see you*'.[7] One's wish for recognition in the sightline of the other is always frustrated because the two looks necessarily fail to coincide. One wants to be looked at, but from the position of an impossible sightline – the imaginary version of one's own. The Lacanian ontology is a universal *méconnaissance* of this kind, a constitutional break or failure, inhabiting every supposed relationship or identification. Lacan developed many different ways of articulating this discord – that between the drive and the object that we saw is examined in *The Ethics of Psychoanalysis* would be one of them – but he would not have been surprised to find Richardson apparently demarcating it along sexual lines.

By the seminar of 1972–73, *Encore*, Lacan had framed this ignorance (or *bêtise*, stupidity) as the very basis of sexual difference, using the talismanic phrase 'there's no such thing as a sexual relationship', Lacan's own 'double yet separate correspondence'.[8] The lack of sexual relationship is created around 'male' and 'female' poles, although most Lacanian practitioners would stress that there is nothing to stop a woman experiencing sexuality in the 'male' fashion or vice versa, and, equally, nothing to exclude homosexual sex from this equation. As Lacan had long maintained, a subject's entrance into language is also the start of its relation to a missing master signifier – 'the phallus' – and the relationship to that absence, he adds here, is what defines the enjoyment of a man and a woman. As Colette Soler helpfully explains:

> A man is the subject who has submitted completely to the phallic function. Consequently, castration is his lot, as well as phallic jouissance, to which he accedes by the mediation of the fantasy ... A woman, on the contrary, is anyone who has *not* submitted *completely* to the regime of phallic jouissance; she has access to an other, supplementary jouissance, without the support of any object.[9]

'Men' submit to a phallus which does not exist and so become founded on a desiring life forever committed to covering over that castrated non-existence with fantasies. 'Women' know full well that the phallus is a fiction, but the cost of this is that their enjoyment is always 'elsewhere', rather than experienced in even fantasised relation to the object at hand. Whatever combination of these forms of jouissance are at work in a given relation between the sexes, the one thing that can be said for them is that they never 'relate': they exist only in their missed collision.

Whether we take Lacan's differentiation of the sexes as empirical fact, a heuristic myth or a therapeutic convenience is not strictly important here. The point is that Lacan is positing a way of thinking about finitude that places sexuality and desire at the heart of being, without imagining that it constitutes a solution. Back in the *Ethics* seminar, Lacan speaks of 'the break that the very presence of language inaugurates in the life of man', adding in *Encore* that 'the subject manifests himself in [t]his gap, namely, in that which causes his desire'.[10] In other words, this gap is not so much something that threatens or disrupts an existing subjectivity but is the prerequisite for entering into subjectivity as such. Going yet further, Alenka Zupančič has called this the 'properly materialistic stance of psychoanalysis', that 'the unconscious is not a subjective distortion of the objective world, it is first and foremost an indication of a fundamental inconsistency of the objective world itself'.[11]

How can we turn this back onto the question of the caesura that instates the tragedy of *Clarissa*? While Clarissa is still at Harlowe Place, Anna provides yet another example of the kind of recurring images of an unbridgeable gulf between

Clarissa and Lovelace we have already seen. Referring to the garden wall that separates them during the period of Clarissa's confinement at Harlowe Place at a point when their correspondence has been interrupted, Anna marvels at the 'but ... *few inches of brick wall* between you so lately; and now such *mountains!*' (C 276); and yet she adds that such a distance would also be the necessary condition of any relationship between them: 'the suiting of the tempers of two persons who are to come together is a great matter: and yet there should be boundaries fixed between them, by consent as it were, beyond which neither should go' (C 277). Richardson and Hill's discussions of the epistolary form as 'a double yet separate correspondence', creating its fine effects out of uncrossable differences, implies that the caesural dimension of *Clarissa* is far more fundamental than even the account in this book as a whole has been able to show. In this novel of the non-relationship, the 'caesura' comes not only in the obvious place of the unnarrated episode of the rape but, like the sexual non-relationship of Lacan's argument, was already there, inscribed as the very condition of its form.

Notes

1 Hölderlin, *Essays and Letters*, p. 318.
2 Richardson, *Correspondence with Aaron Hill*, p. 216.
3 See, for example, Murray L. Brown, 'Learning to Read Richardson: *Pamela*, "Speaking Pictures," and the Visual Hermeneutic', *Studies in the Novel*, 25 (2) (1993): 129–51; and Mary Patricia Martin, 'Reading Reform in Richardson's *Clarissa*', *Studies in English Literature*, 37 (3) (1997): 595–614.
4 Andrew Bennett, *Ignorance: Literature and Agniology* (Manchester: Manchester University Press, 2009), pp. 102, 100.
5 Staves, 'Fielding and the Comedy of Attempted Rape', p. 106.
6 See Macpherson, *Harm's Way*, pp. 13–15.
7 Lacan, *The Four Fundamental Concepts of Psychoanalysis*, p. 103.
8 Jacques Lacan, *Feminine Sexuality: The Limits of Love and Knowledge, 1972–1973*, ed. Jacques Alain-Miller, trans. Bruce Fink (London: Norton, 1999), p. 34.

9 Colette Soler, *What Lacan Said about Women*, trans. John Holland (New York: Other Press, 2008), p. 178.
10 Lacan, *The Ethics of Psychoanalysis*, p. 279; Lacan, *Feminine Sexuality*, p. 11.
11 Zupančič, *Why Psychoanalysis?*, p. 25; the idea is explored further in Slavoj Žižek, *Less than Nothing: Hegel and the Shadow of Dialectical Materialism* (London: Verso, 2012), Chapter 11.

Bibliography

Agamben, Giorgio, *The State of Exception*, trans. Kevin Attell (Chicago, Ill.: University of Chicago Press, 2005).
Alighieri, Dante, *Inferno*, ed. and trans. Charles S. Singleton (Princeton, NJ: Princeton University Press, 1970).
Allan, David, *Commonplace Books and Reading in Georgian England* (Cambridge: Cambridge University Press, 2010).
Auerbach, Erich, *Dante: Poet of the Secular World*, trans. Ralph Manheim (New York: New York Review of Books, 2007).
Barbauld, Anna Letitia, *The Poems*, ed. William McCarthy and Elizabeth Kraft (Athens, Ga.: University of Georgia Press, 1994).
Barchas, Janine, *Graphic Design, Print Culture, and the Eighteenth-Century Novel* (Cambridge: Cambridge University Press, 2003).
Barker, Gerard A., 'The Complacent Paragon: Exemplary Characterisation in *Clarissa*', *Studies in English Literature, 1500–1900*, 9 (3) (1969): 503–19.
——'Clarissa's "Command of Her Passions": Self-Censorship in the Third Edition', *Studies in English Literature 1500–1900*, 10 (3) (1970): 525–39.
Barr, Rebecca Anne, 'Richardson's *Sir Charles Grandison* and the Symptoms of Subjectivity', *The Eighteenth Century: Theory and Interpretation*, 51 (4) (2010): 1–24.
Beebee, Thomas O., *Epistolary Fiction in Europe: 1500–1850* (Cambridge: Cambridge University Press, 1999).
Bender, John, 'Novel Knowledge: Judgement, Experience, Experiment' in Clifford Siskin and William Warner (eds), *This is Enlightenment* (Chicago, Ill.: University of Chicago Press, 2010), pp. 284–300.
Benjamin, Walter, *Selected Writings*, ed. and trans. Marcus Bullock and Michael W. Jennings and others, 4 vols. (Cambridge, Mass.: The Belknap Press, 1996).
——*The Origin of German Tragic Drama*, trans. John Osborne (London: Verso, 1998).
Bennett, Andrew, *Ignorance: Literature and Agniology* (Manchester: Manchester University Press, 2009).

Bennington, Geoffrey, *Sententiousness and the Novel: Laying Down the Law in Eighteenth-Century French Fiction* (Cambridge: Cambridge University Press, 1985).
Binhammer, Katherine, *The Seduction Narrative in Britain, 1747–1800* (Cambridge: Cambridge University Press, 2009).
Broome, Judith, *Fictive Domains: Body, Landscape, and Nostalgia, 1717–1770* (Plainsboro, NJ: Associated University Presses, 2010).
Brown, Murray L., 'Learning to Read Richardson: *Pamela*, "Speaking Pictures," and the Visual Hermeneutic', *Studies in the Novel*, 25 (2) (1993): 129–51.
Budd, Adam, 'Why Clarissa Must Die: Richardson's Tragedy and Editorial Heroism', *Eighteenth-Century Life*, 31 (3) (2007): 1–28.
Bysshe, Edward, *The Art of English Poetry*, 2 vols. (London, 1718).
Canfield, J. Douglas, *Heroes and States: On the Ideology of Restoration Tragedy* (Lexington, Ky.: University Press of Kentucky, 2000).
Castle, Terry, *Clarissa's Ciphers: Meaning and Disruption in Richardson's* Clarissa (Ithaca, NY: Cornell University Press, 1982).
——*The Female Thermometer: 18th Century Culture and the Invention of the Uncanny* (Oxford: Oxford University Press, 1995).
Chartier, Roger, *Inscription and Erasure: Literature and Written Culture from the Eleventh to the Eighteenth Century*, trans. Arthur Goldhammer (Philadelphia, Pa.: University of Pennsylvania Press, 2005).
Connaughton, Michael E., 'Richardson's Familiar Quotations: *Clarissa* and Bysshe's *Art of English Poetry*', *Philological Quarterly*, 60 (2) (1981): 183–95.
Conway, Alison Margaret, *Private Interests: Women, Portraiture, and the Visual Culture of the English Novel: 1709–1791* (Toronto: University of Toronto Press, 2001).
Cook, Daniel, 'Authors Unformed: Reading "Beauties" in the Eighteenth Century', *Philological Quarterly*, 89 (2–3) (2010): 283–309.
Cowley, Abraham, 'The Despair', in *The Collected Works of Abraham Cowley*, ed. Thomas O. Calhoun and others, 6 vols. (Newark, Del.: University of Delaware Press, 1993), vol. II.1, pp. 43–4.
Critchley, Simon and Jameson Webster, *The Hamlet Doctrine* (London: Verso, 2013).
Culler, A. Dwight, 'Edward Bysshe and the Poet's Handbook', *PMLA*, 63 (3) (1948): 858–85.
Damrosch Jr., Leopold, *God's Plots and Man's Stories: Studies in the Fictional Imagination from Milton to Fielding* (Chicago, Ill.: The University of Chicago Press, 1985).
——, *Jonathan Swift: His Life and His World* (New Haven, Conn.: Yale University Press, 2013).

Davidson, Jenny, *Hypocrisy and the Politics of Politeness: Manners and Morals from Locke to Austen* (Cambridge: Cambridge University Press, 2004).

Davis, Gwynn, *Making Amends: Mediation and Reparation in Criminal Justice* (London and New York: Routledge, 1992).

Day, Geoffrey, *From Fiction to the Novel* (London and New York: Routledge, 1987).

Derrida, Jacques, *Of Grammatology*, trans. Gayatri Chakravorty Spivak (Baltimore, Md.: Johns Hopkins University Press, 1997).

——'Freud and the Scene of Writing', in *Writing and Difference*, trans. Alan Bass (London and New York: Routledge, 2001), pp. 246–91.

——*On Cosmopolitanism and Forgiveness*, trans. Mark Dooley and Michael Hughes (London and New York: Routledge, 2001).

Diderot, Denis, *Selected Writings on Art and Literature*, ed. and trans. Geoffrey Bremner (Harmondsworth: Penguin, 1994).

Doody, Margaret Anne, *A Natural Passion: A Study of the Novels of Samuel Richardson* (Oxford: Clarendon Press, 1974).

——'Identity and Character in *Sir Charles Grandison*', in Margaret Anne Doody and Peter Sabor (eds), *Samuel Richardson: Tercentenary Essays* (Cambridge: Cambridge University Press, 1989), pp. 110–32.

Dryden, John and Nathaniel Lee, 'Oedipus: A Tragedy', in *The Works of John Dryden*, ed. H.T. Swedenberg Jr. and others, 20 vols. (Berkeley, Calif.: University of California Press, 1956–2002), vol. XIII, pp. 113–215.

Duyfhuizen, Bernard, 'Epistolary Narratives of Transmission and Transgression', *Comparative Literature*, 37 (1) (1985): 1–26.

Eagleton, Terry, *The Rape of Clarissa: Writing, Sexuality and Class Struggle in Samuel Richardson* (Oxford: Blackwell, 1982).

——*Sweet Violence: The Idea of the Tragic* (Oxford: Blackwell, 2003).

——*Trouble with Strangers: A Study of Ethics* (Oxford: Blackwell, 2009).

Eaves, T.C. Duncan and Ben D. Kimpel, *Samuel Richardson, a Biography* (Oxford: Clarendon, 1971).

EDA Collective, *Twerking to Turking: Everyday Analysis Volume 2*, ed. Alfie Bown and Daniel Bristow (Alresford: Zero Books, 2015).

Empson, William, *Seven Types of Ambiguity* (London: The Hogarth Press, 1984).

——*Using Biography* (London: The Hogarth Press, 1984).

Etherege, George, *The Man of Mode; or, Sir Fopling Flutter*, in J. Douglas Canfield (ed.), *The Broadview Anthology of Restoration and Early Eighteenth Century Drama* (Ontario: Broadview, 2005), pp. 526–89.

Ferguson, Frances, 'Rape and the Rise of the Novel', in R. Howard Bloch and Frances Ferguson (eds), *Misogyny, Misandry, and*

Misanthropy (Berkeley, Calif.: University of California Press, 1989), pp. 88–112.
Fielding, Henry, *Joseph Andrews and Shamela*, ed. Douglas Brooks-Davies and Martin C. Battestin (Oxford: Oxford University Press, 1999).
Flynn, Carol Houlihan, *Samuel Richardson: A Man of Letters* (Princeton, NJ: Princeton University Press, 1982).
Fowler, James, '*La Religieuse*: Diderot's "Richardsonian" Novel', in James Fowler (ed.), *New Essays on Diderot* (Cambridge: Cambridge University Press, 2011), pp. 127–38.
Freud, Sigmund, *The Ego and the Id and Other Works*, ed. and trans. James Strachey (London: Vintage, 2001).
——*The Future of an Illusion, Civilisation and its Discontents and Other Works*, ed. and trans. James Strachey (London: Vintage, 2001).
——*Two Case Histories ('Little Hans' and 'The Rat Man')*, ed. and trans. James Strachey (London: Vintage, 2001).
Furbank, P.N., *Diderot: A Critical Biography* (London: Secker & Warburg, 1992).
Fysh, Stephanie, *The Work(s) of Samuel Richardson* (Newark, Del.: University of Delaware Press, 1997).
Gay, John, *The Beggar's Opera*, in J. Douglas Canfield (ed.), *The Broadview Anthology of Restoration and Early Eighteenth Century Drama* (Ontario: Broadview, 2005), pp. 1332–74.
Gerrard, Christine, *Aaron Hill: The Muses' Projector, 1685–1750* (Oxford: Oxford University Press, 2003).
Goldberg, Rita, *Sex and Enlightenment: Women in Richardson and Diderot* (Cambridge: Cambridge University Press, 1984).
Goldmann, Lucien, *The Hidden God: A Study of the Tragic Vision in the Pensées of Pascal and the Tragedies of Racine*, trans. Philip Thody (London and New York: Routledge, 1964).
Grosvenor Myer, Valerie, 'Well Read in Shakespeare', in Valerie Grosvenor Myer (ed.), *Samuel Richardson: Passion and Prudence* (London: Vision, 1986), pp. 126–32.
Gwilliam, Tassie, *Samuel Richardson's Fictions of Gender* (Palo Alto, Calif.: Stanford University Press, 1993).
Hall, Edith and Fiona Macintosh, *Greek Tragedy and the British Theatre: 1660–1914* (Oxford: Oxford University Press, 2005).
Hammill, Graham and Julia Reinhard Lupton (eds), *Political Theology and Early Modernity* (Chicago, Ill.: University of Chicago Press, 2012).
Hanssen, Barbara, 'Portrait of Melancholy (Benjamin, Warburg, Panofsky)', *MLN*, 114 (5) (1999): 991–1013.
Hardie, Philip, *Rumour and Renown: Representations of Fama in Western Literature* (Cambridge: Cambridge University Press, 2012).

Harris, Jocelyn, 'Richardson: Original or Learned Genius?' in Margaret Anne Doody and Peter Sabor (ed.), *Samuel Richardson: Tercentenary Essays* (Cambridge: Cambridge University Press, 1989), pp. 188–202.

Hays, Mary, *Memoirs of Miss Emma Courtney*, ed. Eleanor Ty (Oxford: Oxford University Press, 2000).

Henning, Standish, 'Branding Harlots on the Brow', *Shakespeare Quarterly*, 51 (1) (2000): 86–9.

Hernandez, Alex Eric, 'Tragedy and the Economics of Providence in *Clarissa*', *Eighteenth-Century Fiction*, 22 (4) (2010): 599–630.

Hilliard, Christopher, *English as Vocation: The Scrutiny Movement* (Oxford: Oxford University Press, 2012).

Hilliard, Raymond H., 'Clarissa and Ritual Cannibalism', *PMLA*, 105 (5) (1990): 1083–97.

Holbrook, David, *English for the Rejected: Training Literacy in the Lower Streams of Secondary Schools* (Cambridge: Cambridge University Press, 1964).

——*The Quest for Love* (London: Methuen, 1965).

Hölderlin, Friedrich, *Essays and Letters*, ed. and trans. Jeremy Adler and Charlie Louth (London: Penguin, 2009).

Huntley, Frank L., '*Macbeth* and the Background of Jesuitical Equivocation', *PMLA*, 79 (4) (1964): 390–400.

Jacobus, Mary, *Psychoanalysis and the Scene of Reading: The Clarendon Lectures in English Literature, 1997* (Oxford: Oxford University Press, 1999).

——*The Poetics of Psychoanalysis: In the Wake of Klein* (Oxford: Oxford University Press, 2005).

Jay, Martin, *Downcast Eyes: The Denigration of Vision in Twentieth-Century French Thought* (Berkeley, Calif.: University of California Press, 1993).

Johnson, Samuel, *The Letters of Samuel Johnson*, ed. Bruce Redford, 3 vols. (Oxford: Clarendon Press, 1992).

——'Life of Cowley', in Roger Lonsdale and John Mullen (eds), *The Lives of the Poets: A Selection* (Oxford: Oxford University Press, 2009), pp. 5–53.

Keymer, Tom, *Richardson's Clarissa and the Eighteenth-Century Reader* (Cambridge: Cambridge University Press, 1992).

——'Clarissa's Death, *Clarissa*'s Sale, and the Text of the Second Edition', *Review of English Studies*, 45 (179) (1994): 389–96.

——*Sterne, the Moderns and the Novel* (Oxford: Oxford University Press, 2002).

Keymer, Thomas and Peter Sabor, *Pamela the Marketplace: Literary Controversy and Print Culture in Eighteenth-Century Britain and Ireland* (Cambridge: Cambridge University Press, 2005).

Klein, Melanie, *Love, Guilt and Reparation and Other Works 1921–1945* (London: Vintage, 1998).

Kramnick, Jonathan, *Actions and Objects from Hobbes to Richardson* (Palo Alto, Calif.: Stanford University Press, 2010).
Lacan, Jacques, *The Ethics of Psychoanalysis*, ed. Jacques Alain-Miller, trans. Dennis Porter (London: Norton, 1992).
——*The Four Fundamental Concepts of Psychoanalysis*, ed. Jacques Alain-Miller, trans. Alan Sheridan (London: Norton, 1998).
——*Feminine Sexuality: The Limits of Love and Knowledge, 1972–1973*, ed. Jacques Alain-Miller, trans. Bruce Fink (London: Norton, 1999).
——*Écrits*, trans. Bruce Fink (New York: Norton, 2006).
Lacoue-Labarthe, Philippe, *Typography: Mimesis, Philosophy, Politics*, ed. Christopher Fynsk (Palo Alto, Calif.: Stanford University Press, 1989).
Lamb, Jonathan, *The Rhetoric of Suffering: Reading the Book of Job in the Eighteenth Century* (Oxford: Clarendon Press, 1995).
Latimer, Bonnie, *Making Gender, Culture, and the Self in the Fiction of Samuel Richardson* (Farnham: Ashgate, 2013).
Leader, Darian, *Why Do Women Write More Letters Than They Post?* (London: Faber & Faber, 1997).
Levin, Gerald Henry, *Richardson the Novelist: The Psychological Patterns* (Amsterdam: Rodopi, 1978).
Locke, John, *A Paraphrase and Notes on the Epistles of St Paul to the Galations, 1 and 2 Corinthians, Romans, Ephesians*, ed. Arthur W. Wainwright, 2 vols. (Oxford: Oxford University Press, 1987).
Loesberg, Jonathan, 'Allegory and Narrative in *Clarissa*', *NOVEL: A Forum on Fiction*, 15 (1) (1981): 39–59.
Loiseau, Jean, *Abraham Cowley's Reputation in England* (Paris: Henri Didier, 1931), pp. 59–62.
Lonsdale, Roger (ed.), *The New Oxford Book of Eighteenth-Century Verse* (Oxford: Oxford University Press, 1984).
Loveman, Kate, *Reading Fictions, 1660–1740: Deception in English Literary and Political Culture* (Farnham: Ashgate, 2008).
McFarland, James, *Constellation: Friedrich Nietzsche and Walter Benjamin in the Now-Time of History* (New York: Fordham University Press, 2013).
McKillop, Alan D., *Samuel Richardson, Printer and Novelist* (Chapel Hill, NC: University of North Caroline Press, 1936).
Macpherson, Sandra, *Harm's Way: Tragic Responsibility and the Novel Form* (Baltimore, Md.: The Johns Hopkins University Press, 2010).
Mann, Thomas, *Doctor Faustus*, trans. H.T. Lowe-Porter (Harmondsworth: Penguin, 1973).
Marsden, Jean I., *Fatal Desire: Women, Sexuality, and the English Stage, 1660–1720* (Ithaca, NY: Cornell University Press, 2006).
Martin, Mary Patricia, 'Reading Reform in Richardson's *Clarissa*', *Studies in English Literature*, 37 (3) (1997): 595–614.

Marvell, Andrew, *The Complete Poems*, ed. Elizabeth Story Donno (London: Penguin, 2005).

Milner, Marion, *On Not Being Able to Paint* (London: Heinemann, 1950).

——*The Hands of the Living God: An Account of a Psycho-analytic Treatment* (London: Hogarth Press, 1969).

Milton, John, *The Complete Poems*, ed. B.A. Wright (London: J.M. Dent & Sons, 1980).

Newman, Jane O., *Benjamin's Library: Modernity, Nation, and the Baroque* (Ithaca, NY: Cornell University Press, 2011).

Nietzsche, Friedrich, *On the Genealogy of Morals*, ed. and trans. Douglas Smith (Oxford: Oxford University Press, 1996).

——*The Birth of Tragedy*, trans. Douglas Smith (Oxford: Oxford University Press, 2000).

——*Ecce Homo*, trans. R.J. Hollingdale (London: Penguin, 2004).

Nussbaum, Felicity A., 'The Unaccountable Pleasure of Eighteenth-Century Tragedy', *PMLA*, 129 (4) (2014): 688–707.

Otway, Thomas, *Venice Preserv'd*, ed. Malcolm Kelsall (London: Edward Arnold, 1969).

Park, William, '*Clarissa* as Tragedy', *Studies in English Literature*, 16 (3) (1976): 461–71.

Paulson, Ronald, *Breaking and Remaking: Aesthetic Practice in England, 1700–1820* (New Brunswick: Rutgers University Press, 1989).

——*Hogarth's Harlot: Sacred Parody in Enlightenment England* (Baltimore, Md.: The Johns Hopkins University Press, 2003).

Plumer, Francis, *A Candid Examination of the History of Sir Charles Grandison* (London, 1754).

Preston, John, *The Created Self: The Reader's Role in Eighteenth-Century Fiction* (London: Heinemann, 1970).

Price, Leah, *The Anthology and the Rise of the Novel: From Richardson to George Eliot* (Cambridge: Cambridge University Press, 2000).

Price, Steven R., 'The Autograph Manuscript in Print: Samuel Richardson's Type Font Manipulation in *Clarissa*', in Paul C. Gutjahr and Megan L Benton (eds), *Illuminating Letters: Typography and Literary Interpretation* (Amherst, Mass.: University of Massachusetts Press, 2001), pp. 115–35.

Raab, Kelley A., 'Creativity and Transcendence in the Work of Marion Milner', *American Imago*, 57 (2) (2000): 185–214.

Reiss, Timothy, *Tragedy and Truth: Studies in the Development of a Renaissance and Neoclassical Discourse* (New Haven, Conn.: Yale University Press, 1980).

Richardson, Samuel, *Clarissa; or, The History of a Young Lady* (London, 1751).

———*Selected Letters*, ed. John Carroll (Oxford: Clarendon Press, 1964).
———*Clarissa; or, The History of a Young Lady*, ed. Angus Ross (Harmondsworth: Penguin, 1985).
———'A Collection of the Moral and Instructive Sentiments, Maxims, Cautions, and Reflections, Contained in the Histories of *Pamela, Clarissa*, and *Sir Charles Grandison*', in *Samuel Richardson's Published Commentary on Clarissa*, ed. Florian Stuber and others, 3 vols. (London: Pickering & Chatto, 1998), vol. III.
———*Pamela; or, Virtue Rewarded*, ed. Margaret Anne Doody and Peter Sabor (London: Penguin, 2003).
———*Clarissa: an Abridged Edition*, ed. Toni Bowers and John Richetti (Ontario: Broadview, 2011).
———*Pamela; or, Virtue Rewarded*, ed. Albert J Rivero (Cambridge: Cambridge University Press, 2011).
———*Early Works*, ed. Alexander Pettit (Cambridge: Cambridge University Press, 2012).
———*Correspondence with Aaron Hill and the Hill Family*, ed. Christine Gerrard (Cambridge: Cambridge University Press, 2013).
———*Correspondence with Sarah Wescomb, Frances Grainger and Laetitia Pilkington*, ed. John Dussinger (Cambridge: Cambridge University Press, 2015).
Rose, Jacqueline, *The Haunting of Sylvia Plath* (London: Virago, 1991).
Rounce, Adam, 'Eighteenth-Century Responses to Dryden's *Fables*', *Translation and Literature*, 16 (1) (2007): 29–52.
Rymer, Thomas, *The Critical Works*, ed. Curt A. Zimansky (Westport, Conn.: Greenwood Press, 1971).
Schulz, Robert M. and Judith Wilt, 'Lovelace and Impotence', *PMLA*, 92 (5) (1977): 1005–6.
Segal, Julia, *Melanie Klein* (London and Thousand Oaks, Calif.: Sage, 2004).
Shakespeare, William, *The Complete Works*, ed. Stanley Wells and Gary Taylor (Oxford: Clarendon Press, 2006).
Sheridan, Frances, *Memoirs of Miss Sidney Bidulph*, ed. Patricia Köster and Jean Coates Cleary (Oxford: Oxford University Press, 1995).
Silk, M.S. and J.P. Stern, *Nietzsche on Tragedy* (Cambridge: Cambridge University Press, 1984).
Siskin, Clifford and William Warner (eds), *This is Enlightenment* (Chicago, Ill.: University of Chicago Press, 2010).
Sitter, John E., 'Mother, Memory, Muse and Poetry after Pope', *ELH*, 44 (2) (1977): 312–36.
Smith, J.A., 'Telling Love: *Twelfth Night* in Samuel Richardson, Teresia Constantia Phillips, and William Blake', *Studies in Philology*, 121 (1) (2015): 194–212.

Soler, Colette, *What Lacan Said about Women*, trans. John Holland (New York: Other Press, 2008).
Spacks, Patricia Meyer, *Gossip* (New York: Knopf, 1985).
—— *Boredom: The Literary History of a State of Mind* (Chicago, Ill.: University of Chicago Press, 1995).
Stallybrass, Peter, Roger Chartier, J. Franklin Mowery and Heather Wolfe, 'Hamlet's Tables and the Technologies of Writing in Renaissance England', *Shakespeare Quarterly*, 55 (4) (2004): 379–419.
Staves, Susan, 'Fielding and the Comedy of Attempted Rape', in Beth Fowkes Tobin (ed.), *History, Gender, and Eighteenth-Century Literature* (Athens, Ga.: University of Georgia Press, 1994), pp. 86–112.
Steiner, George, *Antigones* (Oxford: Clarendon Press, 1984).
Stewart, Elizabeth, *Catastrophe and Survival: Walter Benjamin and Psychoanalysis* (New York: Continuum, 2010).
Swift, Jonathan, *The Complete Poems*, ed. Pat Rogers (Harmondsworth: Penguin, 1983).
——*Gulliver's Travels*, ed. Claude Rawson (Oxford: Oxford University Press, 2005).
——*A Tale of a Tub and Other Works*, ed. Marcus Walsh (Cambridge: Cambridge University Press, 2010).
Tambling, Jeremy, *On Anachronism* (Manchester: Manchester University Press, 2010).
——*Literature and Psychoanalysis* (Manchester: Manchester University Press, 2012).
——'Opera and Novel Ending Together: *Die Meistersinger* and *Doktor Faustus*', *Forum for Modern Language Studies*, 48 (2) (2012): 208–21.
——*Hölderlin and the Poetry of Tragedy: Readings in Sophocles, Shakespeare, Nietzsche and Benjamin* (Brighton: Sussex Academic Press, 2014).
Taylor, E. Derek, *Reason and Religion in Clarissa: Samuel Richardson and 'The Famous Mr Norris of Bemerton'* (Farnham: Ashgate, 2009).
Tierney-Hynes, Rebecca, *Philosophers and Romance Readers, 1680–1740* (London: Palgrave, 2012).
Tricket, Rachel, 'Dryden's Part in *Clarissa*', in Carol Houlihan Flynn and Edward Copeland (eds), *Clarissa and her Readers: New Essays for the Clarissa Project* (New York: AMS, 1999), pp. 175–87.
Warner, William, *Reading Clarissa: The Struggles of Interpretation* (New Haven, Conn.: Yale University Press, 1979).
Watt, Ian, *The Rise of the Novel: Studies in Defoe, Richardson and Fielding* (London: Chatto & Windus, 1957).
Weber, Samuel, *Benjamin's -abilities* (Cambridge, Mass.: Harvard University Press, 2008).

Weigel, Sigrid, *Walter Benjamin: Images, the Creaturely, and the Holy*, trans. Chadwick Truscott Smith (Palo Alto, Calif.: Stanford University Press, 2013).
Weinbrot, Howard D., *Menippean Satire Reconsidered: From Antiquity to the Eighteenth Century* (Baltimore, Md.: The Johns Hopkins University Press, 2005).
Wilt, Judith, 'He Could Go No Farther: A Modest Proposal about Clarissa and Lovelace', *PMLA*, 92 (1) (1977): 19–32.
Wollstonecraft, Mary, *Political Writings*, ed. Janet Todd (London: William Pickering, 1993).
Wright, George T., 'Hendiadys in *Hamlet*', *PMLA*, 96 (2) (1981): 168–93.
Young, Edward, *Night Thoughts*, ed. Stephen Cornford (Cambridge: Cambridge University Press, 1989).
Žižek, Slavoj, *Less than Nothing: Hegel and the Shadow of Dialectical Materialism* (London: Verso, 2012).
Zupančič, Alenka, *The Shortest Shadow: Nietzsche's Philosophy of the Two* (Cambridge, Mass.: The MIT Press, 2003).
——*The Odd One In: On Comedy* (Cambridge, Mass.: The MIT Press, 2008).
——*Why Psychoanalysis: Three Interventions* (Uppsala: NSU Press, 2008).

Name index

Addison, Joseph 8, 15
Adorno, Theodor 149n4
Aesop 140
Agamben, Giorgio 31n33
Alighieri, Dante 107, 117n9, 146
Allan, David 30n18
Aristotle 8, 14
Auerbach, Erich 146

Barbauld, Anna Letitia 132
Barchas, Janine 69, 90n6, 102
Barker, Gerard A. 119n24, 149n6
Barr, Rebecca Anne 152n43
Beebee, Thomas O. 42
Bender, John 28n1
Benjamin, Walter 18–22, 27, 31n40, 67, 68, 74, 82–3, 88, 122, 133–7, 141, 144–9, 149n4, 152–3n58, 154, 155
Bennett, Andrew 156–7
Bennington, Geoffrey 46, 50
Binhammer, Katherine 59
Blake, William 15
Borges, Jorge Luis 72
Broome, Judith 143
Brown, Murray L. 160n3

Budd, Adam 7
Bysshe, Edward 70–1, 83, 86–7, 92n18

Caesar, Julius 104
Canfield, J. Douglas 30n17
Castle, Terry 35, 48, 56, 69, 128, 129–30, 140, 149n6, 152n47
Chartier, Roger 121, 150n20
Chaucer, Geoffrey 37, 110
Cibber, Colley 150n7
Collins, William 76
Connaughton, Michael E. 69–71
Conway, Alison 144
Cook, Daniel 91n11
Cowley, Abraham 68, 84–9, 93n35
Critchley, Simon 30n23
Culler, A. Dwight 69

Damrosch, Leo 9, 61n7
Davidson, Jenny 151n34
Davis, Gwynn 112, 118n19
Day, Geoffrey 90n6
Defoe, Daniel 43, 124

Name index

Derrida, Jacques 42, 115–16, 132
Diderot, Denis 120–1, 148, 149n1
Doody, Margaret Anne 117n3, 125, 151n37
Dryden, John 54–5, 68
Dürer, Albrecht 135, 141, 151n27
Duyfhuizen, Bernard 117n2

Eagleton, Terry 27, 29n11, 62n23
Eaves, T.C. Duncan 62n19
Eliot, George 156–7
Empson, William 63n29, 71
Etherege, George 58
Euripides 15

Ferguson, Frances 112–13
Fielding, Henry 55, 57, 62n20, 112, 139, 157
Flynn, Carole Houlihan 119n24
Fowler, James 149n1
Freud, Sigmund 23–4, 108, 132
Furbank, P.N. 149n1
Fysh, Stephanie 90n6

Garnett, Henry 138
Garth, Samuel 68
Gay, John 58
Gerrard, Christine 150n7
Godwin, William 100
Goethe, Johann Wolfgang von 141
Goldberg, Rita 91n15
Goldmann, Lucien 29n12
Grünewald, Matthias 152–3n58
Gryphius, Andreas 19
Gwilliam, Tassie 143

Hall, Edith 32n53
Hallmann, Johann Christian 19
Hammill, Graham 31n32
Hardie, Philip 36
Hardy, Oliver 147
Harris, Jocelyn 91n10
Hassen, Barbara 135
Hays, Mary 99–100
Hegel, G.W.F 15, 145, 152n53
Henning, Standish 92n28
Hernandez, Alex Eric 7
Hill, Aaron 33, 140n7, 156–7, 160
Hilliard, Christopher 118n14
Hilliard, Raymond H. 119n24
Hogarth, William 134–5, 151n27
Holbrook, David 109–10
Hölderlin, Friedrich 15, 17, 18, 22, 30n22, 31n40, 141, 155
Hume, David 133
Huntley, Frank L. 151n33

Jacobus, Mary 99–100, 118n12
Jay, Martin 6
Johnson, Samuel 29n9, 86, 89
Jonson, Ben 37
Joyce, James 42

Kafka, Franz 147
Keymer, Thomas 10, 29n7, 61n1, 90n5, 90n6, 96, 98, 149n6
Kimpel, Ben D. 62n19
Klee, Paul 20
Klein, Melanie 97, 108–11, 113, 115, 116
Kramnick, Jonathan 9–10, 133, 140

Name index

Lacan, Jacques 22–7, 42, 44, 58, 74, 82, 83, 116, 126, 155, 158–60
Lacoue-Labarthe, Philippe 16, 30n22
Lamb, Jonathan 150n12
Latimer, Bonnie 17
Laurel, Stan 147
Lawrence, D.H. 110
Leader, Darian 42
Lee, Nathanial 54–5, 68
Lennox, Charlotte 62n22
Levin, Gerald Henry 128
Lillo, George 10, 30n17
Locke, John 44–5
Loesberg, Jonathan 119n24
Lohenstein, Daniel Casper von 19
Loiseau, Jean 93n35
Loveman, Kate 61n1
Lupton, Julia Reinhard 31n32
Luther, Martin 20, 31n37

McFarland, James 152n52
Macintosh, Fiona 32n53
McKillop, Alan D. 69
Macpherson, Sandra 9–10, 112, 151n36, 157
Mann, Thomas 88
Marsden, Jean I. 91n15, 92n20
Martin, Mary Patricia 160n3
Marvell, Andrew 86
Mayall, Rik 43
Milner, Marion 109
Milton, John 76
Monteverdi, Claudio 88
Mowery, J. Franklin 150n20
Myer, Valerie Grosvenor 91n10

Newman, Jane O. 19, 31n37
Nietzsche, Friedrich 6, 16, 119n24, 143–6, 152n53, 152n54

Nussbaum, Felicity A. 29n6

Otway, Thomas 13, 16, 68, 72–7, 86, 92n18, 92n21

Park, William 122
Paul 44–5
Paulson, Ronald 134–5, 140, 151n27
Paine, Thomas 6
Plath, Sylvia 71
Plumer, Francis 128–9
Poe, Edgar Allen 42
Pope, Alexander 37
Preston, John 90n5
Price, Leah 30n18, 91n11, 100, 125
Price, Steven R. 90n6
Prévert, Jacques 44

Raab, Kelley A. 118n13
Racine, Jean 9
Radicati, Alberto 133
Raphael 144–5
Reiss, Timothy 8
Rose, Jacqueline 71
Ross, Angus 90n3
Rounce, Adam 91n10
Rowe, Nicholas 72
Rymer, Thomas 8

Sabor, Peter 61n1
Schmitt, Carl 19, 21–2, 31n32
Schopenhauer, Arthur 145
Segal, Julia 118n11
Siskin, Clifford 4
Shakespeare, William 15, 16, 28n2, 36–7, 40, 58, 68, 71, 73, 78–84, 92n21, 92n29, 110, 132
Sheridan, Frances 57

Silk, M.S. 152n54
Sitter, John E. 92n23
Smith, J.A. 92n29
Soler, Colette 158–9
Solomon 49, 56
Sophocles 22, 24–6, 155
Spacks, Patricia Meyer 38–9, 124–5
Stallybrass, Peter 150n20
Staves, Susan 112, 157
Steiner, George 32n53
Stern, J.P. 152n54
Steward, Elizabeth 31n32
Swift, Jonathan 39, 71, 91n11, 132, 138

Tambling, Jeremy 31n40, 37, 38, 93n39, 118n12
Taylor, E. Derek 29n7, 148
Tierney-Hynes, Rebecca 30n16
Tricket, Rachel 56–7
Turner, J.M.W 21

Virgil 47

Warburg, Aby 151n30
Warburton, William 134
Warner, William Beatty 4, 41, 142–3, 149n6
Warton, Joseph 76
Watt, Ian 15, 124, 149n4
Weber, Samuel 20
Webster, Jameson 30n23
Weigel, Sigrid 135, 151n30, 153n58
Weinbrot, Howard D. 62n19
Wescomb, Sarah 41–2
Wilt, Judith 17, 65–6, 67, 95
Wolfe, Heather 150n20
Wollstonecraft, Mary 4–5, 6–7, 28n2, 100
Wright, George T. 92n27
Wright, Joseph 140

Young, Edward 14, 76

Žižek, Slavoj 161n11
Zupančič, Alenka 16, 32n46, 40, 43, 159